Dedicat
My Family & Deacor
First Baptist Church, West

About the book

Written by inspiration of the Holy Spirit.
from life experiences of prayer, praise, consolation, encouragement,
motivation, call to discipleship and
talks with God during the sunset of my life.
May it inspire your path forward.

Cover Artist

Son, Aaron Paul Walker

From the author

Special appreciation to my family for dealing with my urgency to
complete this book as part of my legacy.

THE SUNSET'S BEAUTY
AT THE END OF THE DAY
QUIETS OUR INNER SPIRIT.
INSPIRING US TO LISTEN FOR HIS VOICE
AS WE PRAY WITH PRAISE AND GRATITUDE,
REFLECTING ON ENDINGS ...
ANTICIPATING SUNRISE
WITH CHALLENGING NEW BEGINNINGS.

Scriptural translations,
New Living, New King James,
Life Application Study Bible

Printed USA First Edition Copyright ISBN 978-1-66781-844-3
Inthenightseasons.com
jane rhoda walker

A Gift To

_____

On The Occasion Of

_____

From

_____

Date

_____

Signature in lower case letters
to emphasize "the message"
rather than the "messenger."

jane rhoda walker

Prayers & Praise

Passages And Peace

Encouragement

4

Musings

Occasions

Call To Discipleship

PRAYERS
&
PRAISE

PSALMS 34 1-10 & 18-22 (THE LIVING BIBLE)

I WILL PRAISE THE LORD NO MATTER WHAT HAPPENS.
I WILL CONSTANTLY SPEAK OF HIS GLORIES AND GRACE.
I WILL BOAST OF ALL HIS KINDNESS TO ME.
LET ALL WHO ARE DISCOURAGED TAKE HEART.
LET US PRAISE THE LORD TOGETHER AND EXALT HIS NAME.
FOR I CRIED TO HIM AND HE ANSWERED ME!
HE FREED ME FROM ALL MY FEARS.
OTHERS TOO WERE RADIANT AT WHAT HE DID FOR THEM.
THEIRS WAS NO DOWNCAST LOOK OF REJECTION!
THIS POOR MAN CRIED TO THE LORD...AND THE LORD HEARD
HIM AND SAVED HIM OUT OF HIS TROUBLES.
FOR THE ANGEL OF THE LORD GUARDS AND RESCUES
ALL WHO REVERENCE HIM.
OH, PUT GOD TO THE TEST AND SEE HOW KIND HE IS!
SEE FOR YOURSELF THE WAY HIS MERCIES SHOWER DOWN
ON ALL WHO TRUST IN HIM. IF YOU BELONG TO THE LORD,
REVERENCE HIM; FOR EVERYONE WHO DOES THIS HAS
EVERYTHING HE NEEDS. EVEN STRONG YOUNG LIONS
SOMETIMES GO HUNGRY,
BUT THOSE OF US WHO REVERENCE THE LORD
WILL NEVER LACK ANY GOOD THING.
THE LORD IS CLOSE TO THOSE
WHOSE HEARTS ARE BREAKING.
HE RESCUES THOSE WHO ARE
HUMBLY SORRY FOR THEIR SINS.
THE GOOD MAN DOES NOT ESCAPE ALL TROUBLES...
HE HAS THEM TOO.
BUT THE LORD HELPS HIM IN EACH AND EVERY ONE.
GOD EVEN PROTECTS HIM FROM ACCIDENTS.
BUT AS FOR THOSE WHO SERVE THE LORD,
HE WILL REDEEM THEM;
EVERYONE WHO TAKES REFUGE IN HIM
WILL BE FREELY PARDONED.

FATHER...ONLY YOU

FATHER, ONLY YOU
CAN HOLD ME IN THE PALM OF YOUR HAND.
STRENGTHENING, GRACIOUSLY GIVING ME
THE POWER TO "JUST STAND."
WHEN ALL AROUND ME
SEEMS TO BE JUST CRUMBLING TO THE GROUND.
I STILL TRUST YOU TO MAINTAIN MY MIND...
SANE AND SOUND.
LET ME NOT BE "PUT TO CONFUSION"
TRYING TO INTERPRET
THE DEEP THINGS IN YOUR WORD.
FOR KNOWLEDGE WITH UNDERSTANDING...
WISDOM IS PROMISED...
BECAUSE YOU ARE MY LORD.
IF ANY MAN LACK WISDOM,
THE BIBLE SAYS, JUST ASK
SO, THROUGH YOUR HOLY SPIRIT
WE CAN BE THOROUGHLY
EQUIPPED FOR LIFE'S TASKS.
ONLY YOU CAN GIVE ME COURAGE
TO JUST PRESS ON AHEAD
AS I MAKE ARRANGEMENTS
FOR MEDICAL TREATMENTS
THERE IS NO NEED FOR APPREHENSION OR DREAD.

I NEED NOT FEAR THE ROAD THAT YOU ARE
REQUIRING ME TO TAKE.
FOR YOUR MERCY AND KINDNESS
OVERSHADOWS EACH STEP THAT I MAKE.
I RESUBMIT MYSELF TO THEE...
BOWING HUMBLY
BENEATH YOUR AWESOME POWER,
CONTENT IN THE PRESENCE OF YOUR SPIRIT
TO LEAD AND GUIDE MY EVERY HOUR.
ONLY YOU, FATHER, CAN HOLD ME
IN THE PALM OF YOUR HAND.
STRENGTHENING, EMPOWERING ME
SO THAT WHEN I'VE DONE ALL...
ON YOUR WORD...OF HEALING...
I WILL "JUST STAND."   AMEN

.

PRAYER FOR CONFIDENCE

FATHER, PLEASE DO NOT ALLOW
A SPIRIT OF DISCOURAGEMENT
OR FALSE SENSE OF INADEQUACY,
TO HINDER THE INNER PEACE
THAT YOU'VE ALREADY GRANTED TO ME.
YOU CALLED ME TO YOUR SERVICE LORD,
A LONG, LONG, TIME AGO.
REALITIES OF CONCEPTS
LEARNED IN STUDY WERE REVEALED
AND CONFIDENCE BEGAN TO GROW.
NOT CONFIDENCE IN THINGS
THAT I ACCOMPLISHED ON MY OWN,
BUT GODLY CONFIDENCE
AND YOUR PROMISE THAT I'D NEVER BE ALONE.
THANK YOU, FATHER, FOR THE SPECIAL PLACE
YOU HAVE IN YOUR HEART FOR ME.
THANK YOU FOR YOUR CALL
TO OBEDIENCE THAT ALLOWS
PRAISE AND WORSHIP TO FLOW FREELY.
THANK YOU FOR THE GIFT OF HEALING
THAT HAS DESCENDED FROM YOUR THRONE.
HEALING OF MINDS, SPIRITS, AND BODIES. AS
WE MINISTER TO "YOUR PEOPLE" "IN-HOME."
FATHER, NO MATTER WHAT
SEEMINGLY TRANSPIRES ALL AROUND.
LET ME NOT DEVALUE MY MIND
THAT YOU ALONE...HAVE KEPT SOUND.
I PRAISE YOU...GENTLE MASTER
THAT NEITHER A SPIRIT
OF DISCOURAGEMENT OR INADEQUACY,
CAN SEPARATE ME FROM THE KNOWLEDGE
THAT YOUR SACRIFICE ON
THE CROSS WAS FOR ME.
THAT AS LONG AS I STUDY, ENCOURAGE,
PRAY, WORSHIP, AND WITNESS
ACCORDING TO YOUR HOLY WORD,
YOU'LL DIRECT MY STEPS AND MY PATHWAY
AS YOU ARE MY SAVIOR AND LORD. AMEN

YOUR WILL

FATHER IT IS MORE OBVIOUS TO ME EACH DAY
THAT YOUR WILL ACCORDING TO ME
DOES NOT ALWAYS COINCIDE
WITH YOUR WILL ACCORDING TO YOU.
PLEASE RELEASE ME
FROM A TENDENCY OF ATTEMPTING TO TAKE
CONTROL OF SITUATIONS
THAT SEEMINGLY ARE STUCK ON PAUSE...
NOT MOVING QUICKLY ENOUGH...
PULLING US TOO SLOWLY THROUGH!
YOUR WORD SAYS YOUR PLAN IS FOR GOOD
AND NOT EVIL. GIVING US HOPE AND A FUTURE,
SO, NO NEED FOR ME
TO DRAW THE ROADMAP ON MY OWN...
TO PLACES I THINK I KNOW ABOUT...
BUT IN REALITY, TO ME... ARE UNKNOWN.
MY MANTRA HAS BEEN TRUST, FOR MANY YEARS.
SO COMPLETE TRUST IN YOU IN ALL SITUATIONS
REMOVES ALL FEAR AND ANXIETY.
ALSO, THE REMINDER THAT YOU
ARE NOT
THE AUTHOR OF FEAR, BUT OF POWER,
LOVE AND SOUND MIND
IS CALMING AND KEEPING ME FREE.
FREE FROM TRYING
TO WORK THINGS OUT MY WAY...RIGHT NOW.
PLACING EMPHASIS ON YOU...
THE AUTHOR AND FINISHER OF OUR FAITH
SMOOTHS OUT UNNECESSARY FURROWS ON MY BROW.
SO, FATHER, AS I DAILY
SUBMIT TO YOUR WILL AND YOUR WAY...
"MELT ME, MOLD ME, FILL ME, USE ME.
SPIRIT OF THE LIVING GOD" FALL FRESH TODAY! AMEN.

BLESSING PRAYER

HEAVENLY FATHER, THE YEAR IS PASSING FAST.
BLESS THOSE WHO ARE AWARE
THAT ONLY WHAT IS DONE FOR CHRIST WILL LAST.
BLESS FATHER, THOSE WHOSE
PHYSICAL STEPS ARE SLOWING DOWN.
THOSE WHO ARE LOOKING FORWARD
TO RECEIVING THEIR HEAVENLY CROWN.
THAT CROWN THAT THE SONG SAYS
IS WAITING AND BRIGHT...
IN THE NEW JERUSALEM WHERE FALLETH...NO NIGHT!
BLESS THOSE WHOM
YOU HAVE FILLED WITH YOUR AGAPE LOVE.
THAT LOVE THAT IS EXHIBITED
IN THEIR WALK NOT JUST THEIR TALK.
BLESS FATHER, THE FAMILIES
WHOSE EARTHLY CHAIN HAS BEEN BROKEN...
THE WORD SAYS YOU COMFORT AND HEAL
NO TRUER WORDS HAVE BEEN SPOKEN.
BLESS THOSE FATHER,
WHOSE STEPS ARE NOT DIRECTED TOWARDS THEE.
WHO STILL HAVE NOT ACCEPTED
YOUR TRUTH THAT MAKES THEM FREE.
NOT FREE FROM ALL THE TROUBLES
AND CARES OF THIS WORLD
BUT FREE TO INHERIT YOUR PROMISES
WHEN THEY ACCEPT YOU AS SAVIOR AND LORD.

FREE IN THE KNOWLEDGE
THAT THEY WILL NO LONGER BE ALONE...
FREE IN THE KNOWLEDGE
THAT FOR OUR SINS YOU HAVE ATONED...
FREE TO TALK TO YOU IN PRAYER
AS BOTH THEIR FATHER AND FRIEND.
WHO STICKS CLOSER THAN A BROTHER
ALL THE WAY THROUGH LIFE'S END.
FATHER, I SUBMIT THIS PRAYER
WITH A REQUEST THAT YOU BLESS US
WE...WHO ARE STRIVING
TO LOVE, PRAISE, WORSHIP AND SERVE
ASSURED THAT IN YOU WE'VE PLACED OUR TRUST.
WE'VE ACCEPTED YOU AS OUR PRECIOUS LORD AND SAVIOR
WHICH ENTITLED US TO YOUR HOLY SPIRIT'S
EMPOWERMENT TO CHANGE ATTITUDES AND BEHAVIOR
THAT MAY NOT REFLECT YOU AS FATHER OF US ALL
OR DOES NOT GIVE YOU GLORY
FOR PICKING US UP WHEN WE FALL.
BLESS US TO SPEAK POSITIVITY
INTO THOSE THAT WE MEET...
WITH ENCOURAGEMENT
TO ALL THOSE YOU ALLOW US TO GREET.
BLESS US TO WITNESS OF YOU BY OUR LIFESTYLE.
LET US HASTEN TO DO YOUR WILL,
AS THE SONG SAYS WE MIGHT HAVE "JUST A LITTLE WHILE".
AMEN

OUR RELATIONSHIP

HEAVENLY FATHER, THIS MORNING, I AGAIN THANK YOU
FOR OUR RELATIONSHIP IS THE BEST THING THAT EVER
HAPPENED TO ME. IT ALLOWS YOUR LOVE
TO GO DOWN DEEP IN MY SOUL TO COMFORT, HEAL, AND
FLOW "IN SPITE OF" ENDLESSLY.
SAYING, SINGING, SHOUTING, CRYING,
PRAISE AND THANK YOU CANNOT SUFFICIENTLY
EXPRESS THE POSITIVE EFFECTS OF LIVING THAT
THIS RELATIONSHIP HAS ADDED
TO MY VERY EXISTENCE ON EARTH.
IT ELEVATES MY SELF ESTEEM
AND DESIRE TO DO YOUR WILL
IT REMINDS ME THAT IN YOUR SIGHT
I WILL ALWAYS HAVE WORTH.
EVEN THOUGH MOUNTAINS OF LIFE
AT TIMES APPEAR MUCH TOO STEEP AND TREACHEROUS
TO BE CLIMBED, YOUR WORD GIVES MANIFESTED PROMISES
AND HOPE THAT GROWS VICTORIOUSLY
AS I ASCEND WITH PEACE SUBLIME.
SO YES, HEAVENLY FATHER, I CHERISH
THIS LIFE ENHANCING RELATIONSHIP WITH YOU.
AND VOW TO PRESS
ONWARD AND UPWARD WITH ASSURANCE
THAT YOUR INNER JOY WILL CONTINUE
TO STRENGTHEN ME THROUGH.

POSITIVE STANCE

THANK YOU, HEAVENLY FATHER FOR ANOTHER MORNING
TO GIVE PRAISE AND HONOR TO YOU
FOR SOUND MIND, THE KNOWLEDGE
OF WHO AND WHOSE I AM
FOR REASSURANCE THAT YOU
CONTINUE TO WALK ME THROUGH…
THE UNCERTAINTIES OF LIFE WITHOUT STRESSING…
I'M NOT ONLY WALKING WITH YOU, FATHER,
I AM ACTUALLY STILL PRESSING…
TO PLAY OUT YOUR DESIRED ROLE WHILE NOT ALLOWING
LIFE TO TAKE AN UGLY TOLL
ON MY EMOTIONS, MIND, HEART, BODY OR EVEN ON MY SOUL.

I THANK AND PRAISE YOU ALWAYS AND FOREVER.
CIRCUMSTANCES CANNOT SNATCH ME FROM YOU.
MY STANCE WITH YOU THEY CANNOT SEVER.
SO, THANK YOU, HEAVENLY FATHER
FOR ANOTHER CHERISHED MORNING.
DESIGNED AND ORCHESTRATED BY YOUR LOVE
UNTIL YOU CALL ME TO YOUR HOME ABOVE.
FOR TOMORROWS I NEED NOT FRET, BECAUSE AS MY
OMNIPOTENT FATHER YOU'VE NEVER FAILED ME YET.
YOUR HOLY WORD TELLS ME,
AS THE DAY IS SO SHALL MY STRENGTH BE.
IF I FALTER OR STUMBLE I WILL NOT FALL
BECAUSE YOU LOVE AND PROTECT EXPLICITLY.
YOU ARE NOT A GOD OF CHANCE OR HAPPENSTANCE.
MY WAY IS PREDESTINED.
SO, ON THE MANIFESTATION OF YOUR PROMISES
I CONTINUE TO TAKE A POSITIVE STANCE.

EARNEST PRAYER FOR THIS TIME OF "DEVELOPING THE YOU THAT YOU ARE"

THANK YOU, HEAVENLY FATHER
THAT OUR PHYSICAL PARTS DO NOT DEFINE US.
WE ARE DEFINED BY SOUND MIND AND FAITH
IN OUR GOD IN WHOM WE CONTINUE TO PLACE TRUST.
DECISIONS ARE SUBMITTED IN TOTAL, O GOD.
PLACED WITHIN YOUR DIVINE WILL.
GRANT DISCERNMENT AND INNER PEACE AS
ALL NEEDS YOU CONTINUE TO FULFILL.
FATHER, AS I, THROUGH YOUR WORD,
DEVELOP THE "ME THAT I AM"
WALK WITH ME AS I HESITATINGLY MOVE DOWN PATHS
THAT TAKE ME TOWARD UNFAMILIAR RAMPS...
THAT I MUST TREAD TO REACH
YOUR PRE-DESTINED DEVELOPMENT ROAD.
IN STRICT UNWAVERING FAITH...WHY?
BECAUSE YOU HAVE ALWAYS CARRIED MY LOAD.
THANK YOU, HEAVENLY FATHER, THAT I
WILL ALWAYS BE "COMPLETE IN YOU."
NOT IN SPITE OF CIRCUMSTANCE, BUT IN THEM...
ALLOWING YOU TO WALK ME THROUGH.
THE IMPORTANCE OF THIS FACT, OH GOD,
IS THAT THIS JOURNEY OF DEVELOPMENT?
IS NOT BASED ON OUR PHYSICAL WALK.
IT IS BASED ON OUR SPIRITUAL WALK OF OBEDIENCE
IN OUR DESIRE TO "WALK OUR TALK."
YOU ALONE CAN STRENGTHEN AND ENCOURAGE
WE ARE IN YOUR CARE. ON YOU WE SHALL DEPEND.
THANK YOU, HEAVENLY FATHER,
THAT IN THIS TIME OF DEVELOPMENT
YOU STILL REMAIN MY CLOSEST FRIEND.

PSALM 91:11&15A

FOR HE SHALL GIVE HIS ANGELS
CHARGE OVER THEE,
TO KEEP THEE IN ALL THY WAYS.
HE SHALL CALL UPON ME,
AND I WILL ANSWER HIM:
I WILL BE WITH HIM IN TROUBLE

ONLY BECAUSE
HE
LOVES YOU!

PROTECTIVE POWERS

...I THANK GOD AND GIVE PRAISES TOO...
FOR HIS PROTECTIVE ANGELS
WHOM HE GAVE CHARGE OVER YOU.
HE IS SO WORTHY TO BE GLORIFIED AND PRAISED
HE IS TRUE TO HIS PROMISES
HE'S IN CONTROL NIGHT AND DAY.
HE IS TESTING AND TRYING US...
SO, WE'LL NOT DESIRE TO STRAY.
HE ALLOWED NO HARM TO COME
OR TO SHORTEN YOUR LIFE SPAN.
HE AGAIN PROVED HIS FAITHFULNESS
SO, ON HIS WORD YOU CONTINUE TO LIVE AND STAND.
SO YES, THERE IS SOMETHING ELSE
SPECIAL GOD HAS FOR YOUR LIFE.
JUST CONTINUE TO SEEK...IN HIS WORD...HIS PURPOSE
AS FROM DAY TO DAY YOU STRIVE.

23RD PSALM PRAYER
(Proverbs 16:1,2 LIVING BIBLE)

WE CAN MAKE OUR PLANS,
BUT THE FINAL OUTCOME IS IN GOD'S HANDS.
WE CAN ALWAYS "PROVE THAT WE ARE RIGHT",
BUT IS THE LORD CONVINCED? IS IT IN HIS MASTER PLAN?
I THANK YOU FATHER THAT YOU ARE MY SHEPHERD.
THAT YOU SUPPLY EVERYTHING I NEED.
I THANK YOU THAT WHEN
HIGH TIDES AND STORMS LASH ALL AROUND
YOU LEAD ME BESIDE QUIET STREAMS.
WHEN CIRCUMSTANCES, LOW SELF ESTEEM,
DAILY STRESS OF LIFE OPPRESS ME MORE
THROUGH THE PROMISES AND TRUTHS IN YOUR HOLY WORD,
I AM RESTORED.
WHEN I WALK THROUGH
THE VALLEY OF THE SHADOW
OF DEATH OF LOVED ONES, RELATIONSHIPS, GOALS, DREAMS
I WILL FEAR NO EVIL OR DEPRESSION
FOR THINGS ARE NOT ALWAYS AS THEY SEEM.
YOUR PROMISE TO BE WITH ME
GUARDING AND GUIDING ALL THE WAY...
IS SO UPLIFTING AS YOU ARE MY HOPE AND STAY.
IF PEERS PLAN, CONNIVE, SCANDALIZE MY NAME
YOU PREPARE A TABLE OF STABILITY FOR ME
EVEN IN THEIR PRESENCE YOU REMAIN THE SAME.
I SUBMIT FATHER, TO THE CHASTENING OF YOUR ROD.
AND THE PROTECTION OF YOUR STAFF OF COMFORT
SO NECESSARY AS THE PATHS OF LIFE I TROD.
I'M THANKFUL, OH SO THANKFUL
FOR YOUR GOODNESS AND MERCY
THAT FOLLOWS ME IN MY LIFE.
FOR THE OVERFLOWING OF YOUR INNER PEACE
THAT THE HOLY SPIRIT EMITS
EVEN THROUGH PAINFUL STRIFE.
BEST OF ALL. AFTER YOU HAVE LOVINGLY
SHEPHERDED ME DOWN HERE...
WALKING ME THROUGH TRIALS
AS YOU REMOVE DOUBT
AND CALM ALL FEAR.

I CLAIM THE PROMISE

THAT NO MAN CAN SNATCH,
ME FROM YOU! NO MAN CAN THIS RELATIONSHIP SEVER.
FOR I WILL, NO DOUBT, DWELL WITH YOU
IN YOUR HOME FOR EVER AND EVER.
SO, FATHER, AS WE MAKE OUR PLANS
WE ARE ASSURED
THAT THE FINAL OUTCOME
IS IN ONLY .... YOUR HANDS.
HELP US NOT TO STRIVE
TO "PROVE WE ARE RIGHT"
FOR THE GOOD SHEPHERD
NEEDS NO CONVINCING...
THE FUTURE IS ALREADY IN YOUR SIGHT!!

THANK YOU TODAY

THANK YOU TODAY, HEAVENLY FATHER,
FOR YOUR MERCY AND YOUR GRACE...
FOR PERPETUAL MOTIVATION AND ENERGY
TO DAILY RUN LIFE'S RACE.
THANK YOU FOR YOUR SON
WHO WILLINGLY DIED ON THE CROSS...
TO REDEEM, JUSTIFY AND RESTORE
THOSE WHO WOULD OTHERWISE...BE LOST.
THANK YOU FOR DIVINE PROTECTION
AND GUIDANCE ALONG OUR WAY...
FOR GENTLY REELING US IN
WHEN WE INADVERTENTLY BEGIN TO STRAY.
THE HOPE IN YOUR WORD,
ENLIGHTENS, BRIGHTENS OUR SITUATIONS.
REINFORCING
YOUR UNFAILING LOVE
IN OUR ADVERSITIES...
GIVES US PATIENCE.
SO, THANK YOU,
HEAVENLY FATHER AGAIN
FOR YOUR MERCY AND YOUR GRACE.
MAY WE DESIRE TO WALK HUMBLY
AS WE ADVANCE THROUGH LIFE'S RACE.
AMEN

WE PRAY THAT
**IN QUIETNESS AND CONFIDENCE
SHALL BE YOUR STRENGTH. ISAIAH 13:5**

THANK YOU, HEAVENLY FATHER
FOR A GOOD NIGHT'S SLEEP AND REST.
I NOW SUBMIT THIS DAY UNTO YOU.
ACKNOWLEDGING THAT YOU KNOW WHAT IS BEST.
TO YOU, O HOLY FATHER,
MY LIFE IS AN OPEN BOOK.
THERE IS NO UNKNOWN FOR YOU.
YOUR SOVEREIGNTY REQUIRES NO SECOND LOOK.

I FORGE AHEAD, O FATHER, BY FAITH.
ASSURED THAT MY LIFE
IS PERPETUALLY IN YOUR HAND.
MOLD MY WILL, GRANT PERSEVERANCE,
REINFORCE INNER PEACE AND COMFORT
AS I EXPERIENCE THE UNFOLDING...
OF YOUR "MASTER PLAN."
AMEN

I WILL NOW

BE STILL...

.AND ACKNOWLEDGE

THAT

YOU ARE GOD!

HOPE

WITH JUST A GLIMMER OF HOPE,
WE WOULD TAKE COURAGE AND CARRY ON
DETERMINED TO ENDURE UNTIL THE END.
HOPE IS THE SILVER SHAFT
OF SUN BREAKING THROUGH THE STORM DARKENED SKY,
WORDS OF COMFORT IN A SICK ROOM,
A LETTER FROM A LONG-DISTANCED FRIEND.
HOPE IS THE FIRST SPRING BIRD PERCHED ON A
SNOW-COVERED TWIG AND THE FINISH LINE IN SIGHT.
IT IS A RAINBOW, A SONG, A LOVING TOUCH... WITH BLESSED
ASSURANCE THAT HE ALONE CAN MAKE IT RIGHT.
HOPE SPRINGS ETERNAL, EVERLASTING, ENDLESS, DIVINE.
HOPE LEADS TO INNER PEACE
AND A SPIRITUALLY MADE-UP MIND.
TRUE HOPE GROUNDS US
IN THE KNOWLEDGE OF GOD'S JUSTICE AND IN HIS LOVE
FOR HIS PEOPLE.
THOSE WHO HAVE ACCEPTED
JESUS IN HOMES, ON THE STREETS, OR UNDER HIS STEEPLE.
FIND HOPE IN THE WORD OF GOD.
ASK HIM FOR WISDOM, INTERPRETATION TO INTERNALIZE
DEEP WITHIN YOUR MIND, SPIRIT, HEART AND SOUL
UNTIL IN TIME YOU BECOME
SPIRITUALLY "PERFECTLY WHOLE."

HOPE

O PPORTUNITY TO

PROCEED AND

EVOLVE ON THIS JOURNEY OF LIFE.

CELEBRATION MONTH PRAYER

THANK YOU, FATHER,
SEVENTY- FIVE YEARS AND I'M STILL HERE.
CLOTHED IN MY RIGHT MIND. EXPERIENCING,
SUNSHINE, CLOUDS, STORMS, RAIN AND SOME TEARS.
FATHER I'VE SEEN MORE GOOD DAYS
THAN I HAVE SEEN BAD.
LEARNING TO ACCEPT YOUR COMFORT
HEALS ME WHEN I HAVE BEEN SAD.
YOU HAVE ENHANCED MY VISION
AS YOU ILLUMINATE YOUR WORD.
I'VE EXPERIENCED YOUR PRESENCE
SINCE ACCEPTING YOU AS "MY LORD."
RECOGNIZING AND APPRECIATING
THE SPIRITUAL GIFTS YOU'VE GIVEN ME...
HAS DIRECTED MY THOUGHTS MORE TOWARDS OTHERS
AND TURNED MY EYES MORE TOWARDS THEE.
THIS YEAR HAS BEEN CHALLENGING,
REWARDING. SOME EXPERIENCES HAVE BEEN UNIQUE.
THANK YOU FOR STRENGTH THAT ONLY COMES FROM YOU
WHEN I'M FEELING, UNWORTHY, DOUBTFUL, WEAK.
NOT ONLY IN MY BODY, BUT ALSO IN MY MIND.
SOMETIMES THE HILLS SEEM TO STRETCH EVEN HIGHER
THAT I AM BEING EXPECTED TO CLIMB.
BUT WITH EACH LEVEL
THAT YOU HAVE ADVANCED ME TO,
I'VE EXPERIENCED A NEWFOUND FREEDOM
AND HOLY SPIRIT POWER
WITH AN ASSURANCE OF YOUR PRESENCE,
EACH SECOND, EACH MINUTE, EACH HOUR.

THANK YOU FOR ANOINTED PARENTS
WHOSE PRAYERS YOU ARE ANSWERING...STILL.
THANK YOU FOR SEARCHING MY HEART,
TESTING MY THOUGHTS, FORGIVENESS
AND ACCEPTANCE OF YOUR WILL.
THANK YOU FOR FIFTY-FIVE YEARS WITH MY SOUL MATE.
FOR HIS DIRECTION, PROTECTION, LOVE
WITH EACH STEP THAT WE TOGETHER TAKE.
THANK YOU FOR OUR CHILDREN, THEIR SOUL MATES,
GRANDS, GREAT GRANDS, FRIENDS AND MORE.

THANK YOU, THANK YOU, FATHER,
ENABLE ME TO PRESS ON WITH EXCITEMENT AND DELIGHT.

I CAN'T EVEN IMAGINE
THE GOOD THINGS YOU HAVE IN STORE.
SO, BRING ON THE YEARS
I LIVE IN JOYFUL EXPECTATION
AS I CELEBRATE MY BIRTHDAY MONTH...
CONTINUAL PRAISE AND THANKS,
WILL BE MY CELEBRATION!
HELP ME FATHER TO WALK MY TALK.
TO PICK SOMEONE UP WITH ENCOURAGEMENT OR AID.
TO SHOW MY GRATEFULLNESS TO YOU
FOR THAT FINAL COST THAT FOR US YOU PAID.

PRAYER FOR STABILITY IN OUR STORM...

FATHER, HELP US TO BE STABLE, COMFORTED
AND STRENGTHENED IN "OUR STORM."
WITH ON FIRE, UNWAIVERING FAITH,
NEVER COOL OR LUKEWARM.
STORMS PRESENT IN MANY PHASES
DURING OUR LIFE'S JOURNEY.
OFTEN CALM WITH UNDERLYING
SINK HOLES OR FIERCE WAVES UNCEASINGLY.
HELP US TO DISCERN INVISIBLE SINK HOLES
BEFORE WE GET DRAWN UNDER.
MAY OUR TRUST ACCELERATE WITHIN US
AND NEVER GO USUNDER.
WHEN WE PRAY THANK YOU FATHER FOR YOUR
COMPASSIONATE EAR.
FOR YOU ARE THE AUTHOR OF LOVE AND SOUND MIND
AND A DISPELLAR OF FEAR.
WE OFFER TOTAL PRAISE TO YOU EACH AND EVERY DAY.
CONFIDENT OF YOUR GIFT OF STABILITY, COMFORT
AND STRENGTH ALONG OUR WAY.
SO STABLE, WE CAN BE IN "OUR STORM"
NO MATTER WHAT PHASE SHOWS FORTH.
CONTINUOUSLY EXHIBITING THE FRUIT OF YOUR SPIRIT.
INCREASING INWARD PEACE AND SELF WORTH. AMEN

OBSERVATION

THIS MORNING FATHER,
I LOOK OUT AT THE GREEN GRASS,
THE BIRDS BUILDING NESTS,
THE FLOWERING TREES IN THE YARD...
I'M PRAYING FOR THE FOLKS WHO WALK AND DRIVE BY
WITHOUT ANY APPARENT REGARD...
FOR YOUR EXISTENCE OR THE PENALTY FOR SIN
THAT YOUR SON PAID
SUFFERING AS HE HUNG ON THE OLD RUGGED CROSS
SO THAT ALL OF US COULD BE ETERNALLY SAVED.
HELP US FATHER, TO ACTIVELY RECLAIM
THOSE WHO ARE LOST.
PLEASE DELIVER AND RESTORE THEM
FOR YOUR WORK IS FINISHED ON THE CROSS.
IT IS UP TO US NOW
TO SHARE YOUR GOOD NEWS WITH OTHERS.
TO TELL THEM THAT HOPE FOR THE FUTURE
IS AVAILABLE. FOR IN THEE
WE ARE ALL SISTERS AND BROTHERS.
AS YOUR RESURRECTION DAY
APPROACHES ANOTHER YEAR.
EMBOLDEN YOUR CHILDREN
TO WITNESS FOR YOU WITHOUT FEAR.
YOUR WORD EMPHASIZES THAT WE
A WITNESS MUST ALSO BE.
OUR LIFESTYLE, DAILY WALK
MUST BE PLEASING TO THEE.
SO HAPPY FATHER THAT CHRIST AROSE.
THAT HE DID NOT STAY IN THE GRAVE.
THANK YOU, FOR THE ROAD TO SALVATION
WAS FOREVER DIVINELY PAVED.
HELP US FATHER TO WALK OUR TALK.
TO PICK SOMEONE UP WITH ENCOURAGEMENT OR AID.
TO SHOW OUR GRATEFULLNESS TO YOU
FOR THAT FINAL COST THAT FOR US YOU PAID. AMEN

BOLD PRAISE

HOLY, RIGHTEOUS FATHER,
SOVEREIGN...ABOVE ALL
MY HEART STRINGS ARE BURSTING
IN SONGS OF PRAISE TODAY.
AS GOODNESS, MERCY, GRACE, AND PEACE
ABOUND IN MY LIFE
THERE'S NO REASON TO DESIRE TO STRAY...
FROM YOUR WILL.
STRIVING TO LIVE WITHIN YOUR WORD.
I AM STILL LEARNING TO JUST LEAN ON YOU
INSTEAD OF TO MY OWN UNDERSTANDING.
IN AWE OF THE WAY
YOU ARE CARRYING ME THROUGH.
AWESOME IS A TERM USED BY MANY
IN CONVERSATION. BUT IN MY MIND, IT SHOULD
BE RESERVED FOR YOU ALONE.
TO WHOM CAN WE COMPARE YOUR VIRGIN
BIRTH, DEATH, BURIAL, RESURRECTION AND
ASCENSION TO THE RIGHT HAND
OF THE FATHER ON THE THRONE?
IN CONSTANT AMAZEMENT...I AM...
AS YOU TAKE CARE OF EVEN
THE MINUSCULE DETAILS FOR ME.
YOUR CHILD, WHO AT TIMES DISPLAYS
POOR JUDGEMENT AND OUTRIGHT STUPIDITY!
YOU REINFORCE YOUR COMPASSIONATE
CONTROL OVER A LIFE STRIVING TO LIVE
SPIRIT LED. AS YOU ARE CONSTANTLY
PRUNING AND CHASTISING. URGING ME TO
PRESS ON AHEAD. YOU HAVE HEALED THE
CHILD WITHIN. DELIVERING ME FROM
UNREALIZED GUILT AND FEAR
TO ENJOY AND CHERISH THIS SEASON OF LIFE.
ASSURED THAT YOU ARE ALWAYS NEAR.
IN YOUR WORD ARE ALL THE TOOLS THAT I NEED.
SO, I WILL CONTINUE TO ASK FOR
WISDOM, RENEWED INNER PEACE
WITHIN THIS MIND, BODY AND SOUL
THAT YOU HAVE SO GRACIOUSLY FREED.

ARE WE THERE YET?

OMNISCIENT, OMNIPRESENT,
OMNIPOTENT HEAVENLY FATHER,
WITH SPIRITUAL MATURITY,
KNOWLEDGE OF YOUR HOLY, RIGHTEOUS WORD...
HELP US TO RESET...REBOOT OUR THOUGHTS AND PRAYERS
TO LINE UP WITH YOUR WILL...LORD.
ARE WE THERE YET?

BY YOUR SERVANT ISAIAH
"WHO AM I TO COUNSEL GOD" IS STATED.
THE MANNER IN WHICH WE PRAY
HAS AT TIMES BEEN UNDER RATED.
YES, GOD'S WORD SAYS
WE SHOULD LET OUR DESIRES BE MADE KNOWN
TO AN ALL-WISE GOD WHO SITS HIGH ON HIS THRONE.
ARE WE THERE YET?

IT SAYS WE SHOULD COME
BOLDLY TO THE THRONE OF GRACE.
SCRIPTURAL HISTORY TELLS OF THOSE
WHO EVEN LAID PROSTRATE BEFORE HIS FACE.
ALSO, IT SAYS IF WE ABIDE IN HIM
AND HIS WORD ABIDES IN US
WE CAN ASK ANYTHING, AND IT WILL BE GIVEN
BY THE GOD IN WHOM WE TRUST.
ARE WE THERE YET?

IN FURTHER STUDIES WE ARE TOLD
GOD IS THE TREE AND WE ARE THE BRANCHES.
SO, WE MUST STAY CONNECTED TO HIM
TO MAKE CONTINUAL SPIRITUAL ADVANCES.
KNOWING ALL OF THIS, IT IS NOT A LACK OF FAITH
THAT LEADS US TO SUBMIT FULLY TO GOD'S WILL.

TRUST IN HIM. ACKNOWLEDGE HIM.
LEAN NOT TO OUR OWN UNDERSTANDING,
HE DIRECTS OUR PATH AND DAILY NEEDS HE DOES FULFILL.
ARE WE THERE YET?

WE MUST FOLLOW THE EXAMPLE OF JESUS
IN THE GARDEN OF GETHSEMANE
WHEN HE EXPRESSED TO HIS FATHER GOD
HIS DESIRE TO BE FREE...
FREE FROM THE TORTURED PAINFUL FUTURE
THAT WAS ALREADY DIVINELY LAID OUT BEFORE HIM.
FREE FROM THE PURPOSE OF HIS FATHER
FOR WHICH HE WAS SENT.
HE MOANED, HE PETITIONED, HE WEPT.
THEN THE MOST IMPORTANT WORDS WERE PRAYED.
"NEVERTHELESS, THY WILL BE DONE."
BECAUSE FOR OUR SINS THE PRICE HAD TO BE PAID.
ARE WE THERE YET? NEVERTHELESS, NEVERTHELESS...
HAVE WE REACHED THAT MATURITY YET?
NEVERTHELESS, NEVERTHE LESS IS A PRAYER
WE WILL NEVER REGRET.
AS IT SHOWS FULL, HUMBLE SUBMISSION TO GOD.
HE ALONE THROUGH THE POWER OF HIS HOLY SPIRIT
CAN MOLD OUR MINDS...TO REBOOT...TO RESET....
ARE WE THERE YET?

MY OWN SHOES PRAYER

HEAVENLY FATHER, LET ME BE COMFORTABLE IN SHOES
THAT ARE UNIQUELY MINE.
NOT TO WALK ANYONE ELSE'S MILE
WITH STRINGS THAT TOO TIGHTLY BIND.
YOU ARE ALPHA AND OMEGA
THE BEGINNING AND THE END.
I PRAISE YOU DEAR FATHER.
LET MY FAITH NEVER WAIVER OR BEND.
MIRACULOUS THINGS LET ME EXPERIENCE...
NOT ONLY DAY TO DAY
BUT SECOND BY SECOND YOU ARE THERE
AS YOU POUR OUT CONTINUAL BLESSINGS...
OF YOUR PRESENCE LET ME BE MORE AWARE.
THANK YOU, THANK YOU, THANK YOU,
PRAISES UNENDING, I GIVE.
JUST TEACH ME MORE AND MORE
EVERY DAY WITH YOU IS A PRIVILEGE TO LIVE.
THANK YOU FOR THE YEARS.
THOSE CIRCUMSTANCES YOU HAVE WALKED ME THROUGH
HAVE SHOWN ME IN THE REAL LIGHT OF DAY THAT
YOUR WILL IS THAT I WALK A MILE IN **MY OWN SHOES**.

NO NEED TO COMPARE TO
THE WALK OF OTHERS,
FATHER, MOTHER, AUNTS, COUSINS, UNCLES
SISTERS OR BROTHERS.
AS A **UNIQUE** CHILD OF GOD
HE IS DIRECTING MY INDIVIDUAL PATH
THROWING OUT THE WELL-WORN SHOES
FOR NEW SPIRIT FILLED ONES THAT WILL LAST.

LET ME NOT BE PRESUMTUOUS TO SAY
I'VE BEEN THERE, RIGHT WHERE YOU NOW ARE.
AS EVERY CIRCUMSTANCE HAS VARIENTS
AS DIFFERENT AS GOD'S CELESTIAL STARS.
THANK YOU FOR WORDS OF ENCOURAGEMENT
FROM YOUR HOLY SPIRIT'S PEN.
SOUND WISDOM FROM YOUR WORD
AND EXPERIENCES I'LL NOT NEED TO DEFEND.
LET YOUR PEOPLE BE A WITNESS TO WHAT
WALKING IN YOUR WILL CAN DO...

AWARE THAT YOU OFTEN
DO NOT WALK US AROUND TROUBLES
BUT YOU WILL ALWAYS WALK US THROUGH.
THANK YOU FOR ALLOWING ME TO EXPERIENCE...THE JOY,
THE LOVE CONNECTION ...JUST IN KNOWING...
I CAN BE COMFORTABLE WALKING IN **MY OWN SHOES**
AS YOUR SEEDS OF LOVE, I AM SOWING.

*****

**THE SONG SAYS,
"WALK WITH ME, LORD
WALK WITH ME.
WALK WITH ME, LORD
WALK WITH ME.
ALL ALONG THIS PILGRIM JOURNEY,
I WANT JESUS TO WALK WITH ME"**

A FAITH WALK WITH YOU ...

THANK YOU, FATHER, THANK YOU
FOR THIS FAITH WALK WITH YOU.
WHEN THE WAY IS NOT CLEAR...I NEED NOT FEAR...
FOR THIS MEASURE OF FAITH WILL CARRY ME THROUGH.
WHEN THE CHIPS ARE DOWN AND OTHERS
SMILES ARE REALLY FROWNS
AS THEY CHIP AWAY AT MY SELF ESTEEM.
THANK YOU, FATHER, FOR THIS FAITH WALK WITH YOU
AS THE "SOLE" CAPTAIN OF MY TEAM.
THANK YOU FOR STILL LEADING AS YOU LED THE ISRAELITES.
FOR FAITH ALLOWS ME TO FOLLOW YOUR CLOUDS BY DAY
AND YOUR PILLAR OF FIRE BY NIGHT.
THIS FAITH WALK NOW REFUSES
TO QUESTION THE DEPTH OF YOUR PLAN FOR ME.
IT LOCKS ME IN TO THE MERITS OF FORGIVENESS AND GRACE
PURCHASED BY BLOOD ON CALVARY'S TREE.
THIS FAITH WALK WITH YOU GROWS DEARER AND SWEETER
AS YOU MANIFEST YOUR AWESOME WONDERS.
I CAN ONLY BOW IN HUMBLE SUBMISSION AND PRAISE
IN CONFIDENCE I'LL NOT BE DRAWN UNDER...
BY ANY CIRCUMSTANCE YOU ALLOW ME
TO EXPERIENCE ON MY WAY.
INCREASE MY ZEAL TO STUDY YOUR WORD...
TO TRUST YOU...AND OBEY.
THANK YOU, FATHER, THANK YOU
FOR THIS FAITH WALK WITH YOU.
MAY MY LIFE BE A WITNESS
THROUGH TRIALS AND DISTRESS
THAT ALL PROMISES IN YOUR WORD ...
ARE TRUE.
AMEN

PASSAGES & PEACE

SEASONS AND REASONS

SEASONS AND REASONS FOR ALL THINGS
THAT LIFE TO US WILL BRING.
THE SEASONS ARE APPARENT BUT THE REASONS...
NOT SO MUCH.
AS WE JOURNEY TOWARDS PREDESTINED END
PATIENTLY
WAITING FOR YOUR TOUCH.
THANK YOU AND PRAISE YOU FATHER,
AS YOUR HOLY SPIRIT
EMPOWERS ACCEPTANCE OF YOUR WILL.
GLORY TO GOD IN THE HIGHEST
AS I AM
CLIMBING THIS EARTH'S HIGHEST HILL.
AT TIMES IT HAS BEEN THE "ROUGH SIDE OF THE MOUNTAIN"
BUT THERE NEVER WAS A MOMENT THAT I FELT ALONE
FOR I'VE BEEN ACCOMPANIED BY YOUR ANGELS
SINGING HOLY, HOLY, HOLY ...
PRAISES TO YOU ON YOUR THRONE.
SO NOW I AM HAPPY
IN FACT, JUST ECSTATIC BECAUSE OF YOUR
PROMISE TO BRING ME THROUGH.
HOLD ME CLOSE FATHER TO YOUR BOSOM
UNTIL MY SEASON TO BE WITH YOU.
THE REASON FOR MY REJOICING IS YOUR WORD
TO BE THANKFUL IN ALL THINGS...
SO, I AM LISTENING IN THE DISTANCE...
FOR THE BEAUTY OF THE BELLS OF HEAVEN AS
THEY ...RING…. RING...RING!

OUR DEAR KIND HEAVENLY FATHER

OUR DEAR KIND HEAVENLY FATHER KNOWS US COMPLETELY.
IN SPITE OF THIS KNOWLEDGE,
HE STILL LOVES US UNCEASINGLY.
WE CAN PLACE PAINFUL GRIEF AND
SUFFERING INTO HIS OPEN ARMS.
YOU SEE, OUR STRUGGLING, MOANING, CRYING, EVEN
SCREAMING, DOES NOT CAUSE HIM ALARM.
HE PROMISED US A COMFORTER WHO IS THE HOLY SPIRIT.
HE SUMMONS PEACE AND CALM
WITH STRENGTH TO GO WITH IT.
OPEN YOUR HEART AND MIND'S EYE
TO ACCEPT THIS GIFT OF COMFORT IN LOVE.
LET IT SURROUND YOU TODAY WITH A QUIET STILLNESS
THAT ONLY COMES FROM ABOVE.
YES, OUR DEAR KIND HEAVENLY FATHER
WILL NEVER LET US DOWN.
HE NEVER WILL LEAVE OR FORSAKE US.
HE SUMMONS OUR SMILES TO REPLACE OUR FROWN.
KNOW THAT HE IS GOD.
HIS WORD TELLS US TO JUST KNOW AND "BE STILL".
COMMITING ALL TO OUR DEAR KIND HEAVENLY FATHER.
SUBMITTING TO HIS SOVEREIGN, DIVINE WILL.

JESUS...JESUS...JESUS

JESUS, JESUS, JESUS... IN HIS NAME THERE IS POWER.
JESUS, JESUS, JESUS... HE IS WITH US EVERY HOUR.
ALOUD OR WITHIN OUR SPIRIT,
JUST CALLING ON HIS PRECIOUS NAME
PRODUCES A PEACE THAT PASSES UNDERSTANDING
ALTHOUGH SOME THINGS WILL NEVER BE THE SAME.
LEAVING LOVED ONES MAY SEEM DIFFICULT
BUT WITH HIS STRENGTH...YOU CAN COPE.
ALLOW YOUR HISTORY WITH HIM
TO CONTINUE INCREASING YOUR FAITH AND HOPE...
FOR A FUTURE "KNOWN ONLY TO HIM" CONTROLLED BY A
GOD ON WHOM YOU DEPEND. LONELINESS AND BROKEN-
HEARTS ARE MENDED. THE FUTURE YOU CAN FACE WITHOUT
FEAR AS YOU TRUST FULLY IN JESUS.
CALL ON HIM HE WILL BE FOREVER NEAR.

LET THE WAVES ROLL

"JUST TAKE A DEEP BREATH AND LET THE WAVES ROLL"
WASHING AWAY ALL NEGATIVITY
THAT WOULD LODGE IN YOUR SOUL.
THE CLEAR UNADULTERATED BEAUTY OF SUNSET
IS SO EASILY SEEN WITH THE NAKED EYE.
TAKE A MOMENT TO LOOK INWARD AS YOU
VIEW COLORS OF THE SKY.
ORANGE, RED, PURPLE, GREEN AND GREY .
SPANNING THE HORIZON COMPLETELY...
ABOVE THE ROLLING WAVES...JUST AS IN LIFE'S SEA.
THE TIDE BRINGS IN SAND, STONE,
AND DEPOSITS DEBRIDE,
THEN TAKES OUT WITH IT
SHELLS AND SAND PARTICLES THAT THE EYE CANNOT SEE.
LIFE BRINGS TO US POSITIVES AND NEGATIVES TOO.
WHICH EVER ONE "GROWS" US
IS DEPENDENT ON ME AND YOU.
IT'S ALL A GLORIOUS PART OF GOD'S PERFECT PLAN
ROLLING WAVES AND SIFTING THE SAND
HE CREATED FOR CREATURES AND FOR MAN.

LOSS OF A SIBLING

THE LOSS OF A SIBLING IS UNIQUE IN IT'S DEPTH.
IT'S LIKE NO OTHER EXPERIENCED GRIEF.
ONLY THE HOLY SPIRIT COMFORTER
CAN BRING MUCH NEEDED RELIEF.
EVERY PERSON HAS HAD A DIFFERENT RELATIONSHIP
WEATHER IT IS A SISTER OR A BROTHER.
THE PAIN CUTS DOWN DEEP AND OFTEN MAKES
ONE FEEL AS IF YOU ARE BEING SMOTHERED.
AT TIMES WITH EACH DEEP RELAXATION
BREATH THAT YOU TAKE...
THE TIGHTNESS IN YOUR CHEST IS ENOUGH
TO MAKE YOUR BODY SEEM TO QUAKE.
FAMILY, FRIENDS AND OTHER SIBLINGS
MAY THINK THEY HAVE IT ALL TOGETHER...
THEY MAY THINK BECAUSE THEY'RE A CHRISTIAN
STORMS OF GRIEF ARE EASILY WEATHERED.
THERE IS NO "JUST GET OVER IT" APPLICABLE
TO THIS SPECIAL TYPE OF SADNESS,
CONTINUAL PRAISE AND THANKSGIVING FOR MEMORIES
WILL BRING BACK A GRADUAL GLADNESS.
JUST REJOICING THAT THEY CAME TO KNOW JESUS
AS PERSONAL SAVIOR AND FRIEND
WILL SOMEWHAT EASE THE PAIN OF MISSING THEM
AND REINFORCE THAT YOU WILL MEET AGAIN.
SUBMIT YOUR GRIEF TO OUR SAVIOR,
HE IS WAITING FOR YOUR CALL
FOR HE...THROUGH HIS HOLY SPIRIT
WILL COMFORT...EVEN WHILE TEARS WILL FALL.
HE ALONE CAN DO FOR YOU
WHAT IS MOST NEEDED AT THIS HOUR.
SO... SUBMIT YOURSELF TO OUR SAVIOR
AND EXPERIENCE HIS HEALING POWER.

ON MY WAY BACK HOME

ALL OF MY SICKNESS, ALL OF MY FEARS
HE DID ERASE WITH CLEANSING TEARS
ON MY WAY BACK HOME.
HE NEVER LEFT ME NOR DID HE FORSAKE
ALL OF MY ILLNESS HE DID GLADLY TAKE
ON MY WAY BACK HOME.
I DID NEVER FRET OR FEAR
FOR I FELT MY SAVIOR NEAR.
HE'S RESTORED MY JOY, MY SMILE
WALKING WITH ME ON MY LAST MILE.
MY STEPS ARE FIRM AND I AM SECURE
MY FAITH RENEWED, MY HEART IS PURE
ON MY WAY BACK HOME.
I'M NOW STRIDING WITH MY SAVIOR
HAND IN HAND.
DESTINATION IS THE PROMISED LAND.
ON MY WAY BACK HOME.
IN YOUR SPIRIT WALK WITH ME.
VISUALIZE ME HEALED AND FREE.
RELEASE YOUR WORSHIP AND YOUR PRAISE
HOLY HANDS TO HIM NOW RAISE,
I'M ON MY WAY BACK HOME.
THANK YOU, JESUS, THANK YOU LORD
WE ARE ALL NOW ON ONE ACCORD.
ACCEPTING THE PERFECT WILL OF GOD
FOR AS ON THIS EARTH, YOU TROD...
YOU'RE ON YOUR WAY BACK HOME.

RISE ABOVE THE CLOUDS

HEAVENLY FATHER, HELP US TO RISE ABOVE THE CLOUDS OF
GRIEF THAT OVERSHADOWS US TODAY.
THROUGH YOUR HOLY SPIRIT HELP US TO SEE THAT YOU
HAVE PROVIDED A BETTER WAY.
THAT WE CAN FLY ON THE WINGS OF HEALING FAR ABOVE
THOSE STORMY CLOUDS OF SORROW.
BECAUSE WE HAVE A FUTURE AND
THERE IS ALWAYS NEW HOPE FOR TOMORROW.
THE PEACE OF GOD INSTILLS A CALM
THAT PASSES ALL UNDERSTANDING BY MAN.
IT OVERRIDES THE REALM OF THE IMPOSSIBLE
AND GENTLY WHISPERS…" I CAN...I CAN."
I CAN DO ALL THINGS
THROUGH CHRIST WHO STRENGTHENS ME
TO GO THROUGH THIS GRIEF
WITH A SURE PROMISE OF A BETTER LIFE…
HEALING LASTING THROUGHOUT ..ETERNITY.
A PROMISE THAT NO MATTER HOW DARK THE CLOUDS
BECOME OR HOW LOUD THE THUNDER ROLLS.
HE IS A GOD WHO ACCEPTS OUR THANKS AND PRAISE
AND REMAINS IN DIVINE CONTROL.
OUR MIND DESIRES TO GO AROUND THIS INTERNAL PAIN
INSTEAD OF GLIDING THROUGH…
BUT OUR GOD IS NO RESPECTOR OF PERSONS...
THE RAIN FALLS ON BOTH ME AND YOU.
SO, WE MUST ENCOURAGE OURSELVES.
GOD CAN AND WILL GIVE STRENGTH, RENEWED JOY
TO RISE ABOVE THESE CLOUDS OF SORROW
INTO COMPLETE HEALING.
LET US RESOLVE TO READ HIS WORD, SING HIS SONGS,
PRAISE AND THANK HIM….
FOR "HIS WILL IN CHRIST JESUS CONCERNING YOU".
PUT ASIDE EFFORTS TO UNDERSTAND.
YOU CAN LOVE AND TRUST
DURING YOUR FLIGHT THROUGH GRIEF.
EVER MINDFUL OF THAT PERPETUAL GRIP
THAT HE HAS ON OUR HAND

SILENT SCREAM

TODAY...YES EVEN THIS DAY... GOD OUR
FATHER CAN STILL HEAR OUR "SILENT
SCREAMS" THAT START AT OUR TOES,

CREEP UP THROUGH OUR HEART,

INTO OUR VERY BRAIN, IT SEEMS.

AS IT TRAVELS UPWARD IT GAINS MOMENTUM
AS ANXIETIES START TO RISE

IT CAN EMBODY INSECURITIES, SHOCK, GRIEF,
DEPRESSION, ANGER,

HEALTH ISSUES, DISSAPOINTMENTS TOO...

BUT EVEN IN OUR FUTURE.... FAR... FAR DOWN
THE ROAD. YOU REMAIN IN CONTROL.

WITH NO DIFFIICULTY CARRYING OUR LOAD.

INSTRUCT YOUR HOLY SPIRIT TO MINISTER

TO THAT SCREAM ...WHILE DEEP WITHIN US.

TO ARMOR US UP FOR THE BATTLE THROUGH.

SOVEREIGN GOD IN WHOM WE TRUST.

ENHANCE OUR PRAISE AND THANKS FOR
VICTORIES ALREADY WON,

FOR OUR HISTORY WITH THE FATHER, HOLY
SPIRIT AND ONLY BEGOTTEN SON. THE

ISSUES OF LIFE PROCEED OUT OF THE HEART

SO MOST ESPECIALLY KEEP OUR HEART

IN LINE WITH YOUR DEVINE WILL. INITIATING

RIGHTEOUS GOALS FROM THE START.

YES, GOD OUR FATHER CAN STILL HEAR OUR
"SILENT SCREAM". ALLOWING HIS ANGELS TO
MINISTER PEACE

EVEN WHEN THINGS ARE NOT AS THEY SEEM.

TEARS

PSALM 56: 8-13 TLB
"YOU HAVE SEEN ME TOSSING AND TURNING
THROUGH THE NIGHT.
YOU HAVE COLLECTED ALL MY TEARS
AND PRESERVED THEM IN YOUR BOTTLE.
YOU HAVE RECORDED EVERYONE IN YOUR BOOK.
THE VERY DAY I CALL FOR HELP THE TIDE OF BATTLE TURNS.
MY ENEMIES (CONFUSION, SELF DOUBT, DEPRESSION) FLEE!
THIS ONE THING I KNOW...GOD IS FOR ME!
I AM TRUSTING GOD...OH, PRAISE HIS PROMISES!
I AM NOT AFRAID OF ANYTHING MERE MAN CAN DO TO ME!
YES, PRAISE HIS PROMISES.
I WILL SURELY DO WHAT I HAVE PROMISED, LORD
AND THANK YOU FOR YOUR HELP.
FOR YOU HAVE SAVED ME
FROM DEATH (OF A SOUND MIND) AND FROM
SLIPPING, (AWAY FROM YOU)
SO THAT I CAN WALK (BOLDLY)
IN THE LAND OF THE LIVING!"

THOUGHTS OF GRANDMA AND GRANDPA

IT'S O.K. TO CRY SOMETIME BECAUSE YOU MISS YOUR
GRANDPA AND GRANDMA.
THEN DRY YOUR TEARS QUICKLY.
THEY WOULD WANT YOU TO SMILE ...
BECAUSE GRANDPARENTS LOVE IS FOREVER!
THE BEST WAY TO KEEP THEIR MEMORY ALIVE
WOULD BE TO REGULARLY
CONTINUE TO GO TO CHURCH SCHOOL
AND WORSHIP SERVICES TO CONTINUE
TO LEARN ABOUT JESUS AS YOUR FRIEND.
HIS LOVE WILL HELP YOU REMEMBER THE GOOD THINGS.
THEY WERE HAPPY THAT YOU ACCEPTED JESUS AND WOULD
DESIRE THE SAME FOR ALL OF THEIR GRANDCHILDREN TO
ACCEPT JESUS FOR THEMSELVES
WHEN THEY UNDERSTAND MORE ABOUT HIM.

THE THINGS...

THE THINGS NOBODY TELLS YOU.
THE THINGS THAT YOU'LL GO THROUGH.
THE MOUNTING STACK OF BILLS
THAT QUICKLY COME DUE.
THE TEARS THAT STREAM DOWN OUT OF THE BLUE.
THE DAYS WHEN IT HURTS TO MENTION THEIR NAME.
AND THE DAYS YOU CAN'T STOP SAYING IT
ARE BOTH THE SAME.

WHEN A FLOOD OF EMOTIONS MAKE IT HARD TO MAINTAIN.
AND YOU ASK YOURSELF, "AM I GOING INSANE?"
THE STRUGGLE TO CELEBRATE
MILESTONES WITH OTHERS.
THE BIRTHDAYS, ANNIVERSARIES, THAT FOR YOU
WON'T REACH THOSE NUMBERS.
THE SADNESS YOU FEEL WHILE HAPPY FOR OTHERS.

YOU PRAY FOR EXCITEMENT
AND A SMILE YOU CAN MUSTER. WHEN THE ACHE
IN YEAR SEVEN IS LIKE THAT IN YEAR ONE.
YOU SCREAM TO YOURSELF, "STOP IT!
WHAT'S DONE IS DONE!"

YOU'LL KEEP MOVING FORWARD, BECAUSE LIFE GOES ON.
BUT WHEN YOU'VE LOVED DEEPLY, GONE IS NEVER GONE.
THE TEARS, AFTER YEARS, THAT STILL FALL LIKE NEW.
EMOTIONAL PAYMENTS THAT SUDDENLY COME DUE.
THE THINGS NOBODY TELLS YOU.
THE THINGS NOBODY TELLS YOU.
THE THINGS THAT YOU'LL GO THROUGH.

STRUGGLING TO SING SOME SONGS WITH CONVICTION,
THE WAY THAT YOU USED TO.
WORDS THAT DECLARE 'GOD IS A HEALER',
DON'T SEEM AS CLEARLY TO RING
YOU OPEN YOUR MOUTH, BUT THERE IS NO SOUND.
PASSING THROUGH LIPS
THAT YOUR HURTING HEART HAS BOUND.
WHILE YOU ASK YOURSELF AND GOD,

"WHERE WAS HIS HEALING FOUND?

COULD YOU NOT HEAL HIM ON EARTH?
WHY WAS HE SO SOON HEAVEN-BOUND?"
YOUR MIND KNOWS GOD IS GOOD,
SO, YOU ARE AT PEACE.

BUT IT MAY TAKE A WHILE
FOR YOUR HEART TO RELEASE
AND FULLY ACCEPT GOD'S WILL
AND THE TRUTH OF HIS WORD, AT LEAST.
AND THAT HE'S SOVEREIGN, FAITHFUL
AND HIS LOVE DOES NOT CEASE.

"GOD IS A HEALER." I CAN SING THAT AGAIN
AS I LIFT UP TO HIM MY HURTS, HE HEALS, HE MENDS
GIVING BEAUTY FOR ASHES,
JOY FOR MOURNING, AND THEN
A GARMENT OF PRAISE FOR MY HEAVINESS HE SENDS.

YES, JOYFULLY SING SONGS
THE WAY THAT YOU USED TO
DECLARE THAT GOD IS A HEALER,
WITH CONVICTION, IN TRUTH
IT'S ONE OF THOSE THINGS THAT NOBODY TELLS YOU
IT'S ONE OF THOSE THINGS
THAT YOU CAN MAKE IT THROUGH.

BY PERMISSION VJM

PRECIOUS MEMORIES,
HOW THEY LINGER,
HOW THEY EVER FLOOD MY SOUL.
IN THE STILLNESS
OF THE MIDNIGHT…
PRECIOUS, SACRED
SCENES UNFOLD.

46

RE... I THINK I'LL DROWN IN MY OWN TEARS.

THERE IS A SONG THAT SAYS...
IT BRINGS A TEAR INTO MY EYES
WHEN I BEGIN TO REALIZE
I'VE CRIED SO MUCH
SINCE YOU'VE BEEN GONE
I THINK I'LL DROWN IN MY OWN TEARS.
THAT SONG IS NO LONGER RELATIVE
TO ONE WHOSE LIFE BELONGS TO THE LORD.
BECAUSE HE HAS PROVIDED A "COMFORTER".
IT'S PLAINLY STATED IN GOD'S HOLY WORD.
DON'T MISTAKE MY MEANING.
I'M NOT SAYING WE SHOULD NOT CRY.
WHEN THERE IS GRIEF, SORROW, DISEASE,
GROSS CIRCUMSTANCES AND LIFE'S CLOUDS
ARE DOOM AND GLOOM IN OUR SKY.
THE PSALMIST DAVID
GRIEVED HARD FOR HIS SON ABSALOM.
HE DID NOT EAT, SOCIALIZE OR SLEEP.
BUT WHEN GOD CALLED ABSALOM TO BE WITH HIM
DAVID GOT UP, WASHED HIMSELF
AND BEGAN TO LIVE AND TO EAT.
WHEN A RELATIONSHIP IS DYING OR HAS DIED
TEARS ARE A SAFETY VALVE
TO POUR OUT OUR EMOTIONS AND GRIEF
OF LOVED ONES LOST,
OF RELATIONSHIPS LOST,
OF QUALITY-OF-LIFE LOSS
THAT SNEAKS UP ON US LIKE A THIEF.
GOD'S COMFORT
IS GREATER THAN THE ENEMY'S PLOYS.
WE NEED NOT DROWN IN OUR OWN TEARS.
FOR HIS WORD SAYS
HE IS THE AUTHOR OF SOUND MIND
AND LOVE.
GOD IS NOT THE AUTHOR OF FEAR.

WE NEED NOT FEAR OUR FUTURE
AS WE EXPERIENCE
THINGS WE DON'T UNDERSTAND.
WE CAN SHED OUR TEARS AND PRAY TO GOD
TO GIVE US WISDOM
AND STRENGTH TO STAND.
DROWNING SYMBOLIZES
THAT OUR LUNGS ARE COMPLETELY
FILLED WITH FLUID TO CUT OFF OUR BREATH.
JESUS, THROUGH HIS
SACRIFICIAL CROSS EXPERIENCE
ALLOWS US TO ACCEPT HIM
AND LIVE BEYOND PHYSICAL DEATH.
"HE THAT BELIEVETH ON HIM
SHALL HAVE ETERNAL LIFE."
BELIEVERS ARE FILLED WITH THE HOLY SPIRIT
WHO EMPOWERS US AS WE STRIVE.
SO LET US NOT DROWN
IN OUR OWN TEARS.
EVEN AS WE CRY INTERMITTINGLY
DOWN THROUGH THE YEARS.
GET UP NOW...FEED YOUR BODY
READ GOD'S WORD TO FEED YOUR SOUL.
DO SOMETHING TO HELP OTHERS.
BE ENCOURAGED
THAT YOUR NAME IS ON GOD'S ROLL.
LITTLE BY LITTLE YOU'LL BEGIN TO RECUPE.
TO ENJOY THE SUNSHINE OF LIFE AGAIN.
DON'T BURY YOURSELF
AND DROWN IN YOUR OWN TEARS.
REACH OUT TO JESUS,
HE IS STILL YOUR FRIEND.
HIS LOVE HAS NO LIMIT.
HE POURS OUT
MERCY AND GRACE TO SUSTAIN US
OVER AND
OVER
AND OVER AGAIN.

HEAVEN

NOW JUST THINK OF YOUR HEAVENLY HOME
WHERE WITH JESUS
AND LOVED ONES YOU'LL BE.
WHEN ALL THE BATTLES OF LIFE
HAVE BEEN FOUGHT
AND YOU'VE GAINED YOUR FINAL VICTORY.
WE HAVE READ OF THAT PLACE
WHERE THE STREETS ARE MADE OF GOLD.
WHERE NEW BODIES PREVENT US
FROM EVER GROWING OLD.
WHERE THINGS OF THIS LIFE
THAT GROW UGLY AND TRIVIAL
ARE OUTWEIGHED BY THE FACT THAT
THERE WILL DWELL NO EVIL.
I KNOW YOU LONG TO SEE
YOUR LOVED ONES,
FAMILY AND FRIENDS. SAVED, BAPTIZED BELIEVERS
THAT STRIVE TO PLEASE GOD
TO FOLLOW HIS GUIDE FOR BEHAVIOR.
BY FOLLOWING PRECEPTS
OF OUR SAVIOR AND LORD.
THEY'LL BE SAFE HERE,
THEN BOUND FOR GLORY
TO RECEIVE ETERNAL LIFE AND REWARD.
LIVING LIFE ITSELF GROWS SWEETER
AS FAR AS RELATIONSHIPS GO.
ALSO WITNESSING
GOD'S GRACE AND MERCY
AS IT CONTINUALLY FLOWS.
BUT YES, SOMETIMES JUST THINK OF HEAVEN
WITH JESUS AND LOVED ONES AGAIN.
WITH THE BLESSED ASSURANCE
OF A WORLD
THAT WILL BE WITHOUT END.

SEASON OF BROKENNESS

WHEN YOU ARE WALKING IN BROKENNESS
WITH PIECES OF SORROW, HEALTH CHANGES,
REJECTION, TRIALS
BREAKING APART ALL AROUND,
IT IS THEN...
TIME TO DRAW NIGH TO GOD
SO, HE
CAN PUT THE PIECES BACK TOGETHER
WHILE KEEPING YOUR MIND
STABLE AND SOUND.
WHEN THERE ARE NO WORDS,
SINCERE HUGS
THE PRAYERS OF THE RIGHTEOUS...WILL DO.
IT REINFORCES
THAT YOU ARE LOVED....
THAT OUR GOD
IS WALKING YOU GENTLY THROUGH.
LOSS OF LOVED ONES,
LOSS OF EMPLOYMENT,
LOSS OF HEALTH AND RELATIONSHIPS TOO.
JUST FALL IN THE ARMS OF JESUS
FOR HE LOVES AND CARES FOR YOU.
THE SONG
"FATHER WRAP ME
IN YOUR ARMS AND FATHER ME"
BRINGS COMFORT IN TIMES
OF DISTRESS AND SORROW...
AS YOU ALLOW TEARS TO FLOW...
ALWAYS KNOWING
THAT IN CHRIST
THERE IS HOPE FOR TOMORROW.
THERE IS ONE THING
THAT IS CERTAIN.
ONE IMPORTANT
FACT REMAINS. GOD CAN RESTORE ALL THE PIECES
AND HELP YOU TO SMILE AGAIN.

THE SONG
"FATHER WRAP ME
IN YOUR ARMS AND FATHER ME"
BRINGS COMFORT IN TIMES
OF DISTRESS AND SORROW…
AS YOU ALLOW TEARS TO FLOW…
ALWAYS KNOWING
THAT IN CHRIST
THERE IS HOPE FOR TOMORROW.
THERE IS ONE THING
THAT IS CERTAIN.
INDEED, ONE IMPORTANT
FACT REMAINS. GOD CAN RESTORE ALL THE PIECES
AND HELP YOU TO SMILE AGAIN
IT WOULD SEEM TO BE SO NICE
IF THE BRIDGE OF LOSS
WE WOULD NEVER NEED TO CROSS.
IF WE COULD JUST
KEEP OUR GOOD HEALTH,
OUR LOVED ONES,
RELATIONSHIPS,
AND JOBS…
IF NONE WOULD EVER BE LOST.

BUT THEN WOULD WE MOVE ON IN LIFE
THROUGH THE SEASONS
GOD HAS PLANNED FOR US?
OR WOULD WE JUST
GET STUCK ON SELF SAMENESS.
NOT NEEDING
A GOD IN WHOM TO TRUST?
PERHAPS OUR OCCASIONAL
WALK THROUGH BROKENNESS
DRAWS US CLOSER
TO OUR LORD.

GOD CAN RESTORE ALL THE PIECES
AND HELP YOU TO SMILE AGAIN.
AS WE FEEL OUR STRENGTH RETURNING
WITH POSITIVE TESTIMONY
YES,
OUR GOD
CAN
RESTORE ALL THE PIECES
AND HELP YOU TO SMILE AGAIN.

AS WE FEEL OUR STRENGTH RETURNING
WITH POSITIVE TESTIMONY
AND A SINCERE SMILE
WE ACKNOWLEDGE THAT
GOD
HAS PICKED UP OUR PIECES…
AND
WITH US..
WALKED THAT EXTRA MILE.

JOSHUA 1:5B TLB

**FOR I WILL BE WITH YOU
JUST AS I WAS WITH MOSES.
I WILL NOT ABANDON YOU
OR FAIL TO HELP YOU.**

MAKE MY HEART TO LAUGH AGAIN

FATHER, PLEASE MAKE MY HEART TO
TO LAUGH AGAIN...
FOR YOUR WORD SAYS A BROKEN SPIRIT
SAPS MY STRENGTH WITHIN.
I LONG TO DO YOUR WILL
AS I LIVE OUT MY DAYS.
I AM TRUSTING AND ACKNOWLEDGING
YOU IN ALL MY WAYS...
NOT LEANING TO
MY OWN UNDERSTANDING
SETTLES AND GROUNDS ME
IN YOUR WORD.

FOR YOU HAVE NEVER LEFT ME
SINCE I ACCEPTED YOU AS LORD.
SO, FATHER, I ASK YOU, PLEASE

MAKE MY HEART TO LAUGH AGAIN...

MEND MY BROKEN SPIRIT THAT IS
SAPPING MY STRENGTH WITHIN.
THANK YOU, FATHER, THANK YOU,
THAT THE WORK YOU BEGAN IN ME...
YOU WILL ENABLE AND COMPLETE
BEFORE I REACH ETERNITY.
AMEN

CONTINUE TO HONOR THE MEMORY

THE GREATEST WAY TO HONOR THE

MEMORY OF LOVED ONES GONE HOME IS TO

LOVE THOSE WHOM THEY LOVED.

REJOICE WITH THEIR ACCOMPLISHMENTS & SUCCESSES

AND WEEP WITH THEM ENCOURAGING THEM

THROUGH THEIR DISTRESSES.

TRUE LOVE COMES IN TO EVERYDAY PLAY.

AS YOU CONTINUE

TO BE ON THEIR SIDE EACH AND EVERY DAY

L LAUGH WITH THEM WHEN IN YOUR SPIRIT YOUR HEART
WANTS TO CRY.

O OVERFLOW WITH DISCERNMENT AND PRAISE AS YOU

CONTINUE TO STAND BY THEIR SIDE.

V VIEW THEM AS GOD DOES ...HIS SPECIAL UNIQUE ONES.

E ENERGIZE THEM WITH GOD'S WORD

THANKFUL THAT HE IS THEIR LORD.

WATERS

TURNING AND TOSSING,
BATTLING MY WAY
THROUGH TUMULTOUS WATERS OF GRIEF.
STILL TRUSTING MY LORD AND SAVIOR
UNWAIVERINGLY
FOR HIS PROMISED RELIEF.
SWIMMING,
IN A STEADY OCEAN OF FEELINGS
THAT OVERIDE
REALITY AND EXPECTATIONS
WITHOUT MY SOUL MATE BY MY SIDE.
WADING,
AS THE WATERS GROW CALMER…
LESS RIPPLES WITH INCOMING TIDE.
TREADING,
NEARER STILL NEARER
AS GOD'S WORD IN ME ABIDES.

THE SANDS OF THE BEACH
STRETCHING FROM SUNSET TO SUNRISE.
THE PEBBLES AND SEASHELLS
HAVE SETTLED IN PLACES ALL AROUND.
SYMBOLIZING
THE LOVE OF GOD WHO,
WITH PROMISED COMFORT WILL SURROUND.
I MUST NOW,
ARISE,
ARISE,
ABOVE THE VARIOUS WATERS OF THIS LIFE.
STANDING STRONG, TO BE STILL AND KNOW
THAT I AM WRAPPED
IN THE ARMS
OF THE "LIFEGUARD"
FROM WHOM ALL BLESSINGS FLOW!

DARKEST HOUR

EVEN IN OUR DARKEST HOURS
GOD'S LIGHT IS STILL REFLECTED
IN OUR UNWAIVERING, FAITH FILLED MIND.
HIS LOVE IS GREATER, HIS STRENGTH AND GRACE, A
SUSTAINER, AS ON US,
NEW MERCIES EACH MORNING, HE SHINES.
HIS WORD CONTAINS A PROMISE
TO NEVER LEAVE OR FORSAKE.
EVEN THOUGH DARK, CLOUDY, OCCLUDED SEEMS OUR PATH
HIS PROMISE...HE ...WILL NEVER BREAK.
LOOK UP...LOOK UP...THROUGH THE DARKNESS.
FOCUS ON THE LIGHT THAT STILL SHINES.
ALL SADNESS, APPREHENSION,
SORROW, DEPRESSION OR GRIEF,
THE HOLY SPIRIT CAN EMPOWER US TO OVERCOME
WITH AN UNWAVERING, FAITH FILLED MIND!

NEVERTHELESS

HEAVENLY FATHER, ARE YOU MOVING ME INTO A NEW STAGE
WHERE I AM NO LONGER FREE
TO MAKE DECISIONS OR TO ASSERT WITH MY VOICE?
HAVE YOU CALLED ME TO EVEN RELINQUISH MY CHOICE?
IN GETHSEMANE'S GARDEN
WHEN YOUR SON FACED SURE ADVERSITY
TO THE POINT THAT HIS TEARS WERE EVEN BLOODY
AS HE PRAYED FOR RELEASE.
YOU CALMED HIS FEARS AND GAVE HIM A NEW MINDSET...
"NEVERTHELESS" ... THY WILL IS BEST.
IS "NEVERTHELESS" SECTION OF THIS JOURNEY
JUST UP THE HILL?
WHERE MY RELUCTANCE IS REMOVED SO I CAN SINCERELY
AND WITH NECESSITY BOW AND BEND TO YOUR WILL?
I PRAY DAILY THY WILL BE DONE BECAUSE I BELIEVE WITH
YOUR STRENTH ALL VICTORIES WILL BE WON.
HELP ME TO INTERNALIZE
THE EFFECTIVENESS OF THAT PRAYER.
FOR I DO HAVE BLESSED ASSURANCE
THAT YOU ARE ALWAYS THERE.
YOU'VE ANSWERED PRAYERS
FOR WISDOM IN RESPONSES THAT I MAKE.
YOU HAVE COVERED ME WITH LOVE AND KINDNESS
WITH ENDURANCE FOR THIS RACE.
THE SONG SAYS, NOT TO THE STRONG IS THE BATTLE,
NOR TO THE SWIFT IS THE RACE,
BUT TO THE TRUE AND THE FAITHFUL,
VICTORY IS PROMISED THROUGH GRACE.
THANK YOU, FATHER, FOR GOODNESS
AND MERCY PROMISED IN YOUR WORD
COVERING ALL THE DAYS OF MY LIFE
SINCE MAKING YOU, MY LORD.
NOW I AM ENCOURAGED AS I REMEMBER THAT EVEN JESUS,
YOUR SON, HAD TO YEILD TO
"NEVERTHELESS" FOR HIS BATTLE TO BE WON.
I YIELD, I YIELD, TO THIS
"NEVERTHELESS" STAGE IN LIFE'S JOURNEY.
ASSURED THAT EVEN NOW, AND IN THE FUTURE, I WILL
RECEIVE YOUR PROMISED VICTORY. AMEN

NO RESTING PLACE HERE

DEPRESSION MAY COME.
LET IT NOT FIND A RESTING PLACE HERE.
IT MIGHT ALSO BE FOLLOWED BY SOMETHING WE
EXPERIENCE AS FEAR. LET IT NOT
FIND A RESTING PLACE IN YOU.
NO DAMAGE CAN BE DONE
JUST BECAUSE IT PASSED THROUGH.
ONLY IF WE ENTERTAIN AND ACCEPT IT
ALLOWING IT TO REMAIN.
SO, HERE'S THE WORD...
DEPRESSION, ANXIETY AND FEAR
YOU WILL NOT
FIND A RESTING PLACE HERE!

BE ENCOURAGED BY THE WORD OF GOD
(Excerpts Ephesians 3:14-21)

DO NOT BE OVERWHELMED BY THE
LOSS OF LOVED ONES
OR RELATIONSHIPS HERE ON EARTH.
EVEN THOUGH THEY'VE BEEN
AN INTEGRAL PART OF YOU
THEY STILL DO NOT DETERMINE YOUR WORTH!
YOUR WORTH IS DETERMINED BY
YOUR RELATIONSHIP WITH GOD AND MAN.
AS YOU FACE BATTLES IN THIS LIFE
ON HIS WORD, YOU MUST CONTINUE TO STAND!
"MY THOUGHTS ARE NOT YOUR THOUGHTS
NOR ARE YOUR WAYS MY WAYS,"
SAYS THE LORD IN ISAIAH FIFTY-FIVE EIGHT.
GOD WANTS TO BLESS YOU
FOR THE REST OF YOUR DAYS.
OUR GOD IS NOT CONFINED TO
THE FINITE IMAGINATION OF MAN.
WE FILL OUR MIND WITH PLANNING
BUT HE EXECUTES
HIS MASTER PLAN.
FOR THIS REASON
WE MUST BOW OUR KNEES
TO THE FATHER OF OUR LORD JESUS CHRIST.
FOR WHOM THE WHOLE
FAMILY OF HEAVEN AND EARTH IS NAMED.
HIS HOLY WILL FOR US...
MUST STILL SUFFICE.
OUR DESIRE IS THAT HE WOULD GRANT YOU,
ACCORDING TO
THE RICHES OF HIS GLORY
TO BE STRENGTHENED
WITH MIGHT THROUGH HIS SPIRIT
IN YOUR INNER MAN
AS IF IT WERE MANDATORY.
THAT CHRIST MAY CONTINUE TO DWELL
IN YOUR HEART, THROUGH FAITH.

THAT YOU, BEING ROOTED
AND GROUNDED IN LOVE
MAY BE ABLE TO COMPREHEND
WITH ALL THE SAINTS;
WHAT IS
THE WIDTH, LENGTH, DEPTH, AND HEIGHT.
TO KNOW THE LOVE OF CHRIST
WHICH PASSES KNOWLEDGE.
THAT YOU MAY BE
FILLED WITH THE FULLNESS OF GOD
WITH SPIRITUAL UNDERSTANDING SUPERIOR
TO WHAT IS LEARNED IN COLLEGE.
FOR OUR GOD
IS ABLE TO DO EXCEEDINGLY ABOVE
ALL THAT WE ASK OR EVEN THINK!
ACCORDING TO THE POWER
THAT WORKS IN US...
HIS HOLY SPIRIT IS THE LINK.
TO HIM BE GLORY BY CHRIST JESUS
TO ALL GENERATIONS FOREVER AND EVER...
OUR RELATIONSHIP AND SECURITY IN JESUS,
NO MAN, OR CIRCUMSTANCE...
CAN EVER SEVER.
BE ENCOURAGED BY THESE TRUTHS
AND CONCEPTS
FOUND IN GOD'S HOLY WORD.
BECAUSE THEY DIRECTLY APPLY TO US ALL
SINCE WE'VE ACCEPTED HIM AS LORD.

PRAYER...

**HEAVENLY FATHER, GIVE ME THE GRACE TO BE CONTENT
WITH WHAT YOU GIVE TO ME. NO!
MORE THAN THAT...LET ME REJOICE
THAT YOU ARE WITH ME
IN ALL THAT YOU SEND ME BECAUSE...
IT IS YOUR SOVEREIGN CHOICE.**

THE RAGING STAGE OF GRIEF...

GRIEF WITHOUT A DOUBT
THIS IS THE LONGEST BRIDGE REQUIRED TO CROSS.
WITHOUT A DOUBT
IS THE HIGHEST MOUNTAIN TO ATTEMPT TO CLIMB
THE DEEPEST OCEAN ENDEAVORED TO SWIM,
THE MOST TUMULTUOS WAVES
THAT EVER CRASHED IN SIGHT.
THE FOGGIEST MIST I'VE TRIED TO SEE THROUGH.
THE MOST DEVASTATING SNOWSTORM
WITHOUT A SNOWPLOW.
THE LACK LUSTER BEAUTY OF THE STARS IN THE SKY.
THE DEEPEST DARKEST STORM CLOUDS
THAT HAVE EVER PASSED BY.
THE ROWBOAT MINUS IT'S OARS,
THE SHIP WITH OUT A HUMAN STEERING AT THE HELM.
THE FISHING ROD AND LINE WITH NO BAIT.
THE FLOWERS WITH BUDS AND NO BLOOMS.
THE TREES WITHOUT LEAVES.
SUNRISE AND SUNSET WITHOUT SUN
THE HIGHWAY WITH NO DESIGNATED
MARKINGS OR ROUTE SIGNS.
THE CHURCH WITHOUT IT'S STEEPLE
THE CHOIR STAND WITH NO PEOPLE
JUMONVILLE WITHOUT THE CROSS
FOOD WITHOUT SALT, PEPPER OR SUGAR
A TALL BUILDING WITHOUT AN ELEVATOR
A MICROWAVE WITHOUT ELECTRICITY
AN AIR CONDITIONER WITH NO FREEON
A PENCIL WITHOUT LEAD
A BED WITHOUT A MATTRESS A PRINTER WITHOUT INK
A COLORING BOOK WITH NO CRAYONS
A WORD SEARCH WITHOUT A WORD LIST
AN ENVELOPE WITHOUT A STAMP
A WASHCLOTH WITHOUT SOAP
A BAT WITHOUT A BALL. A LAMP WITHOUT A BULB
TEARS WITHOUT TISSUE. A DOG WITHOUT A BARK
A CAT WITHOUT A MEOW. BIRDS WITHOUT A SONG
CHRISTIAN WITHOUT A BIBLE......
JUST SOME "WITHOUT A DOUBT" RAGING ASPECTS OF GRIEF.

LESS FREQUENT PITY PARTIES

I AM EXPERIENCING LESS FREQUENT PITY PARTIES THAT
GOD ALLOWS FOR THE RELIEF OF STRESS
AS I SETTLE IN TO THE STARK REALITY THAT
GOD ALONE KNOWS WHAT IS BEST.
THESE TEARS I SHED AND THE ANGUISH
OF LOSS I AM FEELING
AT TIMES LEAVES MY BODY JUST ROCKING AND REELING.
LIKE A SHIP CAUGHT OUT IN A SUDDEN STORM
WITH NO WEATHER MAP OR
INSTRUMENT PANEL TO FORWARN
THE SEVERITY OF THE WAVES RUSHING IN
TO CAPSIZE THE SHIP WITH UNRELENTING WINDS.
NO COAST GUARD OR BORDER PATROL RESCUE SHIPS
ON WHOM I CAN DEPEND.
BUT WAIT!
JUST AS SUDDENLY AS THE STORM...
YOU SEND CALMNESS
TO REINFORCE
THE INNER PEACE ALREADY GIVEN.
YOU WRAP ME TIGHTER
IN YOUR COMPASSIONATE ARMS OF LOVE
REMINDING ME THAT
I AM "SPIRIT DRIVEN".
SO, WETHER MY SHIP OF LIFE
VEERS TO THE LEFT OR TO THE RIGHT
YOUR ARMS OF PROTECTION AND GUIDANCE
MUST REMAIN IN MY SIGHT.
SO YES, THESE PITY PARTIES TO RELIEVE STRESS
WILL BECOME LESS FREQUENT TO BE SURE
FOR THERE IS NO QUESTION,
NO ASSUMPTIONS,
NO GUESSES
THAT YOU WILL ALWAYS CARE FOR ME
SO, THERE WILL ALWAYS
BE SPIRITUAL VICTORY!

NOT WITHOUT A SCAR

BROKEN HEARTS WILL HEAL, BUT NOT WITHOUT A SCAR
WE PUT A BANDAIDE ON IT. A BANDAIDE OF NUMBNESS,
ANGER, ACCEPTANCE, REALITY.
THAT COVERS AND STOPS THE ACTIVE BLEEDING BUT
LEAVES A SCAR OTHERS CANNOT SEE.
WE ENGAGE IN ACTVITIES THAT ARE ORDINARY AND
RENEWING EVEN WITH A SMILE.
BUT MEMORIES OF LOVED ONES LOST WITH WHOM WE
TRAVELED THEIR LAST MILE
CONSTANTLY FILL THE MIND, LOSSENING THAT BAND AIDE
UNTIL IT FINALLY DROPS AWAY
LEAVING A HUGE UGLY SCAR THAT WILL FOREVER STAY.
THE SILENT WOUND
MIGHT EVEN FESTER BEFORE IT HEALS COMPLETELY.
ALLOWING THOUGHTS OF DISEASE AND IT'S PROCESS TO
OVER RIDE THE HAPPIEST AND BEST MEMORIES.
GOD SENT US HIS HOLY SPIRIT TO AID US THROUGH THIS
GRIEF PROCESS BUT STILL SENDS US THROUGH
SO, THROUGH WE MUST GO,
SINCE THERE IS NO WAY AROUND.
TIME IS A HEALER OF SOME THINGS.
AS WE PRAISE STRIVING FOR POSITIVITY
WE ARE COVERED WITH GRACE, PROTECTION,
PROVISIONS, GOODNESS AND MERCY
ALLOWING EVEN A SCARRED HEART.
TO STILL SING!

THE EXPERIENCE OF NUMBNESS....

NUMBNESS IS A PROTECTION THAT ALLOWS US TO SLOWLY
REACT AND ADJUST TO REALITY.
IT ALLOWS OUR MIND TO
SLOWLY CATCH UP WITH OUR EMOTIONS AND BODY.
NUMBNESS IS A FLOW
THAT PUTS US IN NO PARTICULAR STAGE OF GRIEF
AS IT'S FLOW IS NOT MANDATED BY YOU.
AS IT FLOWS YOU WILL FIND YOURSELF
EASING IN TO THE REALITY OF WHAT WAS SUDDENLY
FORCED UPON YOU EVEN IF YOU FELT THAT YOU WERE
PREPARED. THERE IS NO PREPARATION
FOR THIS TYPE OF GRIEF. BAM!   YOU'RE IN IT!!!
ACCEPT ALL THE HELP MADE AVAILABLE.
GRIEF IS A "WE" BATTLE......NOT A "ME" BATTLE
WE HURT TOGETHER, CRY TOGETHER, LAUGH TOGETHER
PRAY TOGETHER AND TOGETHER ACCEPT THE INNER PEACE
PEACE THAT PASSES ALL UNDERSTANDING...NO MATTER
WHAT IT BRINGS WE MUST ALLOW OUR HEART TO STILL SING.

ALONE

WE CAN FEEL ALONE
EVEN IN THE MIDST OF A CROWD
WHEN THE MOST IMPORTANT
HUMAN IN OUR LIFE IS MISSING.
NO MATTER THE LENGTH OF TIME!
IT'S NOT THE LONELINESS
IMPLIED IN "I WILL NEVER LEAVE OR FORSAKE YOU"
IT IS SIMPLY BECAUSE
THE PIECE OF THE PUZZLE
THAT MADE IT COMPLETE
IS MISSING IN OUR TIME AND SPACE.
SO AS WE ABSORB, ADJUST, ACCEPT THIS GRIEF
THAT HAS FOREVER ALTERED OUR LIFE AND OUR BEING.
WE MUST CONTINUE TO
CLING TO OUR FATHER AS
WE WALK THROUGH OUR PREDESTINED LIVES HERE
"ALONE" ... BUT NOT ALWAYS LONELY.

PSALM 87:7B "ALL MY SPRINGS ARE IN THEE"

"ALL MY SPRINGS ARE IN THEE...LORD
REFRESHING SPRINGS ACCORDING TO THY WORD.
SPRINGS OF CONTENTMENT AND INNER PEACE...
SPRINGS OF COMFORT AND COMMUNION WITH THEE...
SPRINGS OF SATISFACTION IN TRUSTING YOUR WORD...
SPRINGS OF KINSHIP AS AN HEIR OF THINE...LORD...

THANK YOU FOR YOUR REFRESHING SPRINGS
SWEET, COOL, AND EVER FLOWING.
THANK YOU FOR ACCESS TO THEM
AND A GOD WHO IS...ALL KNOWING.

GOD'S ROLL

HEAVENLY FATHER,
FRIENDS, ACQUAINTANCES AND LOVED ONES NAMES
ARE BEING CALLED FROM YOUR ROLL.
LIVES ARE MORE QUICKLY VANISHING
AS THE BELLS OF DEATH SWIFTLY TOLL.
OH, FATHER, LET US NOT TAKE LIGHTLY
YOUR VISIBLE WARNING SIGNS.
LET US ALLOW YOU TO WIPE OUR SLATES CLEAN.
GRANT CONTINUED INNER PEACE
AND A GOD CENTERED MIND.
WE HAVE THE ASSURANCE, FATHER,
THAT IN DEATH WE'RE JUST MOVING ON.
NO NEED TO FEAR OR TREMBLE AS
WE REST ON YOUR PROMISES TO NEVER LEAVE US ALONE.
WE'VE READ THAT HEAVEN IS A BEAUTIFUL PLACE OF PEACE.
WHERE WE CAN REJOICE WITH THE ANGELS
WHOSE PRAISES HOLY, HOLY, HOLY
TO YOUR NAME WILL NEVER CEASE.
BEFORE OUR DAY COMES, OH FATHER
LET US NOT ALLOW ANYTHING BETWEEN
YOU AND US OR MAN AND US…
THAT WILL PREVENT OUR
VIEWING THOSE BEAUTIFUL SCENES.
HELP US TO WITNESS TO OTHERS.
THERE IS NO MORE TIME FOR DELAY…
TO ACKNOWLEDGE YOU AS PERSONAL SAVIOR,
FOR YOUR FACE WE SHALL SEE ONE DAY.
I AM NOT RUSHING YOUR TIME, FATHER
OR TRYING TO FORESEE YOUR MASTER PLAN.
I'M JUST MORE AWARE OF THE SURETY
THAT IT'S INEVITABLE THAT WE'LL LEAVE THIS LAND.
SO, LET THIS BE THE SEASON
FOR PROMPT FORGIVENESS AND AGAPE LOVE.
A SEASON OF CONTINUAL SINCERE PRAISE TO YOU
AS DO THE ANGELS IN HEAVEN ABOVE.

THE ONLY HUG THAT MATTERS

IT DOES NOT MATTER THAT THE HUG THAT
ENGAGES ME IS WITH STRONG ARMS.
IT CAN NEVER MATCH OR COME CLOSE TO THE HUGS
THAT KEPT ME FROM EVER BEING HARMED.
IT CAN NEVER MEAN TO ME,
"I LOVE YOU WITH A LOVE THAT IS ENDLESS"
OR THAT "AS LONG AS I LIVE ON THIS EARTH
I WILL NEVER EVER BE FRIENDLESS"
IT CAN NEVER MEAN "I WILL LOVE AND CHERISH YOU "
AS WAS SPOKEN IN OUR SACRED VOWS.
IT CAN NEVER MEAN "NOW AND FOREVER"
WITH AN ARCH IN THE BROW.
IT'S HARD TO EVEN FATHOM
THE LOSS OF THOSE STRONG ARMS.
TO EVEN HAVE TO RELY ONLY
ON MEMORIES OF YOUR HIDDEN CHARMS.

OH, IT'S ALL ABOUT THE HUG I DID NOT GET TODAY.
FOR THE FIRST TIME IN SIXTY-TWO YEARS

CIRCUMSTANCES HAVE TAKEN YOU AWAY.

TO A PLACE I COULD NOT PROVIDE,

TO A PLACE PRIORITIZING HEALTH AND SAFETY.

A PLACE WHERE BECAUSE OF COVID 19 RULES,

I AM NOT PERMITTED.

A PLACE WHERE YOU ARE UNABLE TO ROAM FREELY.

GOD IS STILL IN DIVINE CONTROL

AND HAS PROVIDED A WAY FOR US

TO ENGAGE IN THAT STRONG ARMED HUG

NOT FACE TO FACE BUT VIRTUALLY.

TIME IS FLEETING NOW, RUNNING IT'S COURSE OF LIFE.

I NEED TO SAY I AM STILL SO BLESSED BY YOUR HUGS

AND TO BE YOUR FAITHFUL, LOVING WIFE.

ALWAYS & FOREVER JANE

A REFLECTIVE LOOK IN THE MIRROR

OH, I LOOKED INTO THE MIRROR AND WHAT DID I SEE??
THERE WAS AN UNFAMILIAR OLD LADY STARING BACK AT ME.
BLOND HAIR RETURNED TO ITS NATURAL WHITE.
THAT PLEASANT NATURAL SMILE HAD BEGUN TO FLEE.
HAD I REALLY NOT LOOKED IN THE MIRROR
FOR WELL OVER A YEAR?
SEEMS LIKE A STRANGER TOOK MY PLACE...
FULL OF GRIEF AND TEARS.
WHERE DID THE TIME FLY?
WHAT HAPPENED TO A SATISFIED FULFILLING LIFE?
WHAT LEFT ME SO ALONE AND EMPTY?
WHAT THREW ME INTO THIS UNEASY PLIGHT?
OH, I REMEMBER NOW... IT WAS LOSS.
LOSS OF HOME THAT SUDDENLY BECAME JUST A HOUSE.
LOSS OF TRUE LOVE
AND COMPANIONSHIP THAT I HAD IN MY SPOUSE.
LOSS OF DREAMS AND PLANS FOR OUR RETIREMENT YEARS.
LOSS OF AN ABILITY TO PROCEED
THROUGH LIFE WITHOUT FEAR...
FEAR OF BEING DRAWN UNDER INTO A DEEP DARK HOLE
OF EMPTINESS AND INCOMPLETION
OF MY USUAL LIFE'S ROLE.

BUT WAIT, BEHIND THAT HIDEOUS REFLECTION
THERE SEEMS TO REFLECT A RAY OF HOPE.
SOMEWHERE, THERE'S A GLIMPSE OF SPIRITUAL SCOPE.

THERE'S A PROMISE RECALLED
THAT "I WILL NEVER LEAVE OR FORSAKE YOU"
I WILL PROVIDE MIRACLES WAY OUTSIDE OF YOUR VIEW.
YOU ARE PART OF AN ONGOING HISTORY WITH ME.
THAT BEGAN WHEN I DIED FOR YOU
AND SET YOUR SOUL FREE.
LOOK UP…. LOOK UP…BEYOND YOUR HAIR,
GRIEF STRICKEN AND STRESSFILLED FACE.
GIVE ME THAT TOTAL PRAISE FOR MY MERCY,
.
YES, GIVE ME THAT TOTAL PRAISE
FOR MY MERCY STRENGTH, AND GRACE.
DISMISS THAT PITY PARTY FOR WHICH I HAD NO INVITATION.
ENHANCE THAT DANCE OF PRAISE
I GAVE WITH YOUR SALVATION.
LET THAT MIRROR BECOME YOUR DEAREST FRIEND.
LET THAT FACE REMIND YOU OF
WHERE YOU HAVE ONCE BEEN.
TO THE MOUNTAIN TOP LOOKING OVER THE OTHER SIDE.
WITH THE COURAGE AND JOY OF THE LORD
STRENGTH AND GODLY PRIDE
IN ALL YOU'VE BEEN BLESSED WITH.
THE GOALS YOU WERE PERMITTED TO ATTAIN.
BY TRUST IN THE LIVING GOD,
OMNIPOTENT,
OMNISCIENT,
WHO FOREVER IN YOUR LIFE REIGNS!

STRENGTH FOR THE DAY

ONE OF THE PROMISES IN GOD'S WORD
IS STRENGTH FOR THE DAY.
AS WE WALK THIS PAINFUL SEASON OF GRIEF
FAITH AND TRUST IS THE ONLY WAY.
DO NOT BEND OVER WITH THE WEIGHT OF CARE.
YOU'VE ALREADY CAST THEM ON JESUS.
THOSE BURDENS HE WILL GLADLY BEAR.
LOOK UP, LOOK UP TO THE GOD
WHO GAVE HIS ONLY SON.
HE IS FAMILIAR WITH YOUR PAIN.
ASSUREDLY HE ADDRESSES THEM ONE BY ONE.
YOU ARE NOT THE ONLY ONE EXPERIENCING
PAIN, SICKNESS, DISAPPOINTMENTS
WHILE TRAVELING IN THIS LAND.
GOD RESTORES, REPLENISHES YOUR STRENGTH
AS ON HIM ONLY...YOU CONTINUE TO STAND.
THIS GRIEF ROAD IS ONE
OF THE HARDEST TO TREAD...
EVEN OUR LORD JESUS CHRIST WEPT
WITH A BOWED DOWN HEAD.
HE SAID "I AM THE GOD WHO HEALS"
WHEN HE DIED ON THE CROSS.
ASSURING US OF SALVATION
NO SAVED SOULS WILL BE LOST.
SO, GATHER AROUND FAMILY
AND FRIENDS TOO.
AS YOU PRAY AND PRAISE TOGETHER
THE HOLY SPIRIT GENTLY WALKS YOU THROUGH.
LIFT UP YOUR HEAD AND HANDS
IN PRAISE AND THANKS TO OUR SAVIOR
AS HE STRENGTHENS AND GUIDES YOU IN GRIEF
WITH A RENEWED THANKFUL BEHAVIOR.
JUST CONTINUE TO READ AND STUDY HIS WORD...
ENCOURAGED BY MANIFESTATION OF THE PROMISES
ENTITLED TO YOU SINCE YOU ACCEPTED HIM AS LORD.
SUNSET WEEPING IN SORROW IS TIMELESS AND
PAR FOR THE COURSE
BUT SUNRISE JOY OF HEALING COMFORT FOLLOWS
BECAUSE JESUS THE CHRIST IS YOUR SOURCE.

OUR FATHER, GOD IS SPECIAL

OUR FATHER, GOD IS SPECIAL
FOR OUT OF CONFUSION, HE BRINGS PEACE.
HE SPEAKS CALM INTO OUR SITUATIONS,
EMITTING AN INNER JOY THAT WILL NEVER CEASE.
HE HAS AN EYE TO SEE THE FUTURE.
HE CAN SOFTEN AND WARM A HEART
THAT IS HARDENED AND COLD.
HE SPEAKS LIFE INTO OUR CIRCUMSTANCES.
GENTLY GUIDES THOSE OF US YOUNG OR OLD.
OUR FATHER GOD IS A HEALER OF MIND, BODY AND SOUL.
HE FULFILLS PROMISES IN HIS WORD AND RECORDS OUR
NAME ON HIS ROLL.
HE SENT HIS SON TO EARTH
TO GIVE HIS LIFE FOR YOU AND ME.
HE PAID THE COST FOR OUR SINS,
SO, FOR ALL, ETERNAL LIFE IS FREE
HE DOES NOT BEAT US INTO SUBMISSION.
THROUGH HIS WORD HE WOOES EACH ONE.
HE IS THE HEAD OF THE GODHEAD...
HOLY SPIRIT AND THE SON.
ONE HAS ONLY TO BELIEVE AND RECEIVE.
CONFESSING THAT BELIEF WITH THEIR MOUTH.
ASKING FORGIVENESS FOR ALL HAVE SINNED
OUR HEAVENLY FATHER SAVES AND BRINGS US OUT.
OUT OF LIFE'S DARKNESS
INTO HIS MARVELOUS LIGHT.
ACCEPT, TRUST AND OBEY. LIVING ACCORDING TO HIS WORD
WILL SUFFICE. IN A WORLD
OF SO MUCH TRAGEDY AND CONFUSION
ONLY OUR SPECIAL FATHER GOD CAN BRING PEACE.
ONLY HE CAN TURN OUR
MOURNING INTO GLADNESS
WITH A JOY THAT EMITS PEACE.

ANOTHER THANK YOU, HEAVENLY FATHER

THANK YOU, HEAVENLY FATHER
FOR YOUR MERCY AND YOUR GRACE.FOR A
PORTION OF ENERGY TO KEEP STEADY IN LIFE'S RACE.
ENERGY THAT NOT ONLY COMES
FROM PHYSICAL STRENGTH.
IT ALSO COMES FROM BOUNTIFUL SPIRITUAL BLESSINGS
THAT GO BEYOND LENGTH.
I AM RENEWED
BY THE BEAUTY OF YOUR FLOWERS, BUTTERFLIES,
THE SONGS OF YOUR BIRDS ALONG THE WAY.
THE RISING SUN AND
SPECTACULAR SUNSETS YOU PROVIDE FOR US EACH DAY.
THE HAWK GLIDING IN THE SKY IN TRIOS OR ALONE.
THE BUNNIES, SQUIRRELS, TURKEYS
AND DEER THAT SO FREELY ROAM.
THANK YOU, AGAIN HEAVENLY FATHER, FOR FAMILY,
FRIENDS, GOODNESS, MERCY AND GRACE.
ALL ARE UPLIFTING AND ENCOURAGING AS
I JOURNEY THROUGH TIME AND TOWARDS SPACE.
MY STATUS AS "A FIXER"
HAS BEEN CHANGED TO THAT OF A MANAGER
OF THE PLANS THAT HAVE
BEEN DIVINELY ARRANGED FOR ME.
SO AS YOUR NATURE CALLS TO MY ATTENTION
YOUR CARE FOR EVEN THE LITTLE SPARROW
IT ENHANCES SECURITY ON LIFE'S JOURNEY
KNOWING AND ACCEPTING
THAT IN YOUR WILL...**WHAT WILL BE WILL BE**.
CONTINUE TO GUARD MY HEART
FROM WHICH FLOWS THE ISSUES OF LIFE,
MY THOUGHTS, MY TONGUE,
MY ACTIONS, MY HOPES AND DREAMS
EVEN WHEN LIFE UNFOLDS DIFFERENTLY THAN IT SEEMS.
YES, THANK YOU, HEAVENLY FATHER,
FOR YOUR MERCY AND GRACE,
I WILL CONTINUE TO THRIVE
ON THE ENERGY YOU HAVE PROVIDED FOR LIFE'S RACE.

REFLECTIONS OF CONVERSATION WITH A SPOUSE DEMENTIA CAREGIVER ...MIND TO HEART....

SO HOW DO I GET THE FACTS IN MY MIND
TO BE ACCEPTED IN MY HEART?
HOW DOES IT COMPUTE IN MY BRAIN TO THE EXTENT
THAT I CAN START SHAPING MY LIFE AROUND
CIRCUMSTANCES THAT NEVER REMAIN THE SAME?
FEELING A NEED TO BE ON HAND
FOR EVERY MOVEMENT OF LIFE'S GAME.
THIS GAME OF LIFE THAT HAS BEEN
DEALT TO ME AND MY MATE.
I REALIZE WE ARE IN THE HANDS OF GOD
JUST WALKING DAY BY DAY BY FAITH.
SOME FACTS ARE VERY OBVIOUS TO OTHERS
BUT DIFFICULT FOR ME TO BELIEVE.
I DO BELIEVE THE WORD OF THE LORD...
BUT WHAT I EXPERIENCE IS HARD TO RECEIVE.
THE WORD OF THE LORD GOD,
MY FATHER, CONTINUES TO SAY...
I'LL BE WITH YOU NOW AND ALWAYS
JUST TRUST OBEY AND PRAY.
SO, I PRAY THAT I CAN INTERNALIZE REALITY.
STILL AWARE OF THE FATHER'S MIRACLES
THAT HAVE DIRECTLY AFFECTED ME.
I PRAY THAT I WILL NOT JUST LET LIFE FLY BY UNLIVED....
WHILE I'M LOCKED INTO MY DREAMS, WHAT I DESIRE
FATHER HELP ME TO BE CONFIDENT,
TRUSTING THAT YOUR WILL BE DONE
WHILE ENJOYING THE FREEDOM
THAT I KNOW HAS BEEN HEAVEN SENT.
SO, HOW DO I GET THE FACTS IN MY MIND
TO BE ACCEPTED IN MY HEART.
I'LL TURN IT OVER AGAIN TO MY FATHER AND TAKE
ADVANTAGE OF AN ENLIGHTENED START.
"LOOK AND LIVE, MY SISTER LIVE,
LOOK TO JESUS NOW AND LIVE.
IT'S RECORDED IN HIS WORD...HALLELUJAH
IF ONLY YOU WILL LOOK AND LIVE.

CONTINUED REFLECTIONS

HON, HON, WHERE ARE YOU?

YOU'RE LYING BESIDE ME...
YOU'RE NINETY YEARS OLD NOW...BUT WHERE ARE YOU?
SIXTY-FIVE YEARS WE WERE SO HAPPY, SO FREE
I LOOK INTO YOUR TWINKLING EYES
AND I KNOW YOU'RE STILL HERE
BUT CHANGES IN YOUR MIND SET
ARE CAUSING MORE AND MORE TEARS.
STRONG, GENTLE, HUMOROUS, LOVING, DEPENDABLE
ALL POSITIVE ASSETS OF "HON" ...TIL NOW.
SOME EXHIBITED BEHAVIORS
PUT A FROWN TO MY BROW.
HON, HON, WHERE ARE YOU?
YOU TELL ME THANKS, AND "YOU LOOK PRETTY"
AS YOU SMILE YOUR MISCHIEVOUS SMILE,
LIFE AGAIN SEEMS SO NORMAL
AS WE TREAD TOGETHER OUR SENIOR MILES.
THEN SOMETHING STRANGE COMES OVER YOU
AND YOU...I RECOGNIZE...NOT AT ALL.
CANTANKEROUS, EDGEY, NON-APPROVING
UNCOOPERATIVE WAVES ROLL OVER YOU...
ANYTHING I DID NOT ASK
IS EXACTLY WHAT YOU WANT TO DO!
THIS DREADFUL DISEASE CALLED ALZHEIMERS
HAS MOVED IN TO OUR ADDRESS.
BUT OUR GOD IS GIVING ME
EXCEPTIONAL STRENGTH TO PASS THIS PRESENT TEST.

HE REMINDS ME THROUGH HIS SPIRIT
THAT PROMISES IN HIS WORD ARE STILL TRUE.
THAT NO MATTER WHERE YOUR MIND GOES
HIS HOLY SPIRIT REMAINS IN YOU.
THOUGH MY QUESTION, HON WHERE ARE YOU?
STILL ROLLS OVER AND OVER IN MY HEAD.
GOD GIVES ME REASSURANCE THAT
THERE IS NO NEED TO DREAD.
BECAUSE HE KNOWS THE PLAN.
YES, THE PLAN THAT HE HAS FOR US.
NOT FOR EVIL...BUT A HOPE AND A FUTURE!
SO, FOR BOTH OF US...I WILL CONTINUE TO TRUST.
AS THE SONG SAYS... JESUS LOVE IS STILL...
RICHER, FULLER, DEEPER...

YES, JESUS LOVE IS STILL SWEETER...
HIS LOVE IS SWEETER
AS THE YEARS GO BY!!
SO, PRAYERS AND PRAISE ASCEND TO HIM
THROUGH SMILES AND THROUGH TEARS.
I'LL NOT LEAN TO MY OWN UNDERSTANDING
I'LL ACCEPT HIS DIRECTION THROUGH OUR YEARS
Written for Callie 2013

NOVEL OF LIFE

WHEN LIFE'S NOVEL BEGINS TO READ LIKE A MYSTERY.
THE MIND HAS A TENDENCY
TO TRY TO "FIGURE IT OUT". BUT WHEN I WENT TO GOD'S
WORD, I FOUND THAT SOME
MYSTERIES ...TO MAN... WILL REMAIN UNKNOWN FOR IN HIS
WILL...WHAT WILL BE WILL BE.
THE SONG SAYS...GOD WORKS IN MYSTERIOUS WAYS HIS
WONDERS TO PERFORM.
HE PLANTS HIS FOOTSTEPS ON THE SEA
AND RIDES UPON THE STORM.
THE HOLY SPIRIT HAS A UNIQUE WAY OF FREEING MY MIND
FROM QUESTIONING CHAPTERS

WHILE LIVING LIFE'S BOOK OF MYSTERIES
HE SPEAKS PEACE THRU THE SITUATIONS,
STILLING MY MIND, REMOVING STRESS AND AGITATION
THAT AT TIMES...ACCOMPANIES SOME VERSES AND
PARAGRAPHS OF LIFE .
REENFORCING THAT THEY ARE
COMPLETELY OUT OF MY CONTROL.
HE HAS A WAY OF GENTLY
PUSHING ME INTO SUBMISSION TO ALMIGHTY GOD'S WILL
TO REALIZE I MUST WORK MY FAITH TRUSTING THAT ALL
NEEDS HE WILL CONTINUE TO FULFILL.

IT IS LIKE A "BLESSED QUIETNESS" AS HE SPEAKS
CONTENTMENT TO MY SOUL
WHILE RELEASING TUMULTUOUS WAVES OF DISTRESS.
SATAN STILL TRIES TO DULL MY VICTORIES BY
ENTERING MY THOUGHTS WITH
UNCERTAINTY AND DREAD.
BUT PRAYER IS THE KEY, FAITH UNLOCKS THE DOOR
TO THE EVIDENCE OF THINGS UNSEEN.
WORSHIP AND PRAISE NOW FLOODS MY SOUL WITH
CONFIDENCE LIKE A GENTLY RUNNING STREAM.
THE STREAM THAT EVOLVED
FROM AN OCEAN OF HOPE TO A RIVER OF TRUST
IN OUR TRUE AND LIVING GOD WHO DAILY MINISTERS TO US.
REFILLING EACH NOOK AND CRANNY THAT FLOWS
NOW INTO A BROOK
OF A HISTORY OF DIVINE INTERVENTION...

SO NOW I TAKE A SECOND LOOK...A NEW LOOK,
A REFRESHED, REJUVENATED LOOK
THROUGH THE PAGES OF LIFE
AS I LIVE EACH LETTER
AND EACH LINE.
I AM SECURE IN THE KNOWLEDGE
THAT AS I WALK IN THE WILL OF GOD....
NO MATTER HOW MANY PAGES ARE IN LIFE'S NOVEL...
ALL WILL CONTINUE TO BE FINE!

ENCOURAGEMENT

ACTIVELY WAIT

AT TIMES, DO YOUR TROUBLES LOOM LARGER AND GREATER
THAN YOU THINK YOU CAN BEAR?
COULD IT BE
THAT YOU ARE MINIMIZING THE POWER
OF OUR SOVEREIGN GOD...
WHO IS ALWAYS AWARE
OF THE COMPLEXITIES OF OUR BODIES,
INTRICASIES OF OUR MIND...
THE SENSITIVITIES OF OUR CHARACTER
AND THE WEIGHT OF
RELATIONSHIP TIES THAT BIND.
THE PROPHET ISAIAH SAYS,
HAVE YOU NOT KNOWN, HAVE YOU NOT HEARD?
THE EVERLASTING GOD,
THE CREATOR OF THE ENDS OF THE EARTH
NEITHER FAINTS, NOR IS WEARY.
A REMINDER OF HIS WORTH!
HE GIVES POWER TO THE WEAK AND INCREASES
STRENGTH TO THOSE WHO HAVE NO MIGHT.
AS EVEN THE YOUTH
FAINT AND BECOME WEARY,
YOUNG MEN WILL UTTERLY FALL
BUT WE STILL NEED NOT THINK
WE ARE LOSING LIFE'S FIGHT.
THIS IS A PROMISE.
THOSE WHO ON THE LORD WILL WAIT
SHALL BE ENDOWED WITH NEW STRENGTH...
THEY SHALL MOUNT UP
WITH WINGS AS EAGLES.
THEIR SUCCESS IN LIFE
IS NOT MEASURED BY LENGTH.
THEY SHALL RUN AND NOT BE WEARY.
THEY SHALL WALK AND NOT FAINT.
SO HAVE FAITH,
TRUST, OBEY AND PRAY
THESE ARE ACTION WORDS...
RESOLVE NOW...TO JUST **ACTIVELY WAIT**

SPIRITUAL DEMOLITION

FATHER, THE SPIRITUAL DEMOLITION TRUCK
IS BIDDING FOR A NEW JOB SITE...
TO TEAR DOWN RELATIONSHIPS,
SELF-CONFIDENCE, INNER PEACE
THAT WAS NEVER CONTROLLED BY MIGHT.
YOUR WORD SAYS, "NOT BY POWER NOR BY MIGHT
BUT BY MY SPIRIT SAITH THE LORD."
SO, NO MATTER WHAT DESTRUCTIVE METHODS ARE USED
THERE IS REBUILDING,
RESTORATION AND HEALING IN GOD'S WORD.
SOME OF THE CRACKS IN SPIRITUAL WALLS
BEGIN AS JUST HAIRLINE INSULTS AND VERBAL ABUSE.
THEN LIES, DECEPTION,
MANIPULATIONS WIDENED THE CRACKS
TO THE EXTENT THAT THE WALLS HAD NO USE.
UNGODLY ACTIONS ERODED THE FOUNDATION
THAT HAD ONCE BEEN VERY STRONG...
THEN THE BLOCKS BEGAN TO FALL
WHEN THERE WAS NO ADMISSION OF WRONG.
THE ROOF INSTEAD OF A PROTECTIVE COVERING
BECAME LEAKY AND FULL OF HOLES.
THE STORMS OF LIFE JUST BADGERED IT
UNTIL IT NO LONGER PLAYED ITS PROTECTIVE ROLE.
BUT...OH...THE BLOOD OF JESUS STEPPED IN WITH
FORGIVENESS, HEALING, REBUILDING FOR THE SOUL!
IT COVERED THE ROOFTOPS WITH GRACE, MERCY AND LOVE,
ENABLING THE HOLY SPIRIT TO REFOCUS OUR LIVES
ON THE GOD WHO REMAINS IN CONTROL.
HE FILLED THE HAIRLINE CRACKS
OF INSULTS, VERBAL ABUSE AND DECEPTION
WITH MANIFESTATION OF GOD'S PROMISES
TO ALL WHO WILLINGLY ACCEPTED SALVATION.
THE WIDER CRACKS
EROSION OF SELF ESTEEM
WERE FILLED WITH REASSURANCE THAT
"ONCE FOR ALL" WE'VE BEEN REDEEMED.

SO, WE SPIRITUALLY RECONNECT TO OUR UNIQUENESS
GIVEN BY GOD BEFORE OUR BIRTH...
PRAISING AND THANKING OUR HEAVENLY FATHER
FOR REINTERNALIZATION OF OUR WORTH.

SO YES, CALL OFF THE BID
FROM THE DEMOLITION CREW.
AND DON'T REFER THEM TO SOMEONE ELSE
WHO IS STRUGGLING TO GO THROUGH.
THE RECONSTRUCTION COMPANY LED BY OUR GOD
WHOSE ONLY SON PAID THE COST FOR US
HAS DONE ITS JOB SECURING OUR SPIRITUAL BUILDING
WHILE REIGNITING A NON– WAVERING TRUST!

PROVERBS 4:4,5,6
THE LIVING BIBLE (EDITED)

HE TOLD ME NEVER TO
FORGET HIS WORDS.
IF YOU FOLLOW THEM, HE SAID,
AND DEVELOP GOOD JUDGEMENT
AND COMMON SENSE,
I CANNOT OVEREMPHASISZE THIS POINT.
CLING TO WISDOM...
SHE WILL PROTECT YOU.
LOVE HER...SHE WILL GUARD YOU.
DETERMINATION TO BE WISE
IS THE FIRST STEP TOWARD
BECOMING WISE! AND WITH YOUR WISDOM,
DEVELOP COMMON SENSE AND GOOD
JUDGEMENT. IF YOU EXALT WISDOM, SHE WILL
EXALT YOU. HOLD HER FAST AND SHE WILL LEAD YOU TO
GREAT HONOR; SHE WILL PLACE A
BEAUTIFUL CROWN UPON YOUR HEAD.
MY DAUGHTER, LISTEN TO ME
AND DO AS I SAY
AND YOU WILL HAVE A LONG LIFE.

THE UNHEALED CHILD WITHIN

IS THERE STILL AN UNHEALED CHILD
BURIED DEEPLY WITHIN US….
THAT HINDERS FULL SURRENDER TO
THE GOD IN WHOM WE'VE PLACED OUR TRUST?
HAS OUR WITNESS BEEN AFFECTED BY THIS
UNHEALED CHILD WITHIN?
DOES THIS CHILD KEEP REMINDING US
OF WHERE OUR LIVES HAVE BEEN?
HAVE WE NOT INTERNALIZED
THAT OUR SINS HAVE BEEN
CAST "AS FAR AS THE EAST IS FROM THE WEST?"
IF WE HAVE ASKED GOD FOR FORGIVENESS
HIS HOLY SPIRIT AIDS US THROUGH LIFE'S TESTS.
AS CHRISTIANS THE SPIRIT THROUGH GOD'S WORD
MAKES US BRAND NEW OUTSIDE AND INSIDE
WHILE GIVING US DAILY WISDOM SO IN THAT
WORD WE CAN ABIDE.
WE ARE NOT REFORMED, REHABILITATED,
OR RE EDUCATED.
WE ARE RECREATED! OLD THINGS HAVE PASSED
AWAY. UNGODLY BEHAVIORS HAVE BEEN ABATED.
OUR TRUST IN CHRIST ALLOWS US…
OUR SIN…FOR HIS RIGHTEOUSNESS TO EXCHANGE.
UNDER THE CONTROL OF HIS SPIRIT
EVEN PRIORITIES HAVE BEEN REARRANGED.
OUR SIN WAS POURED INTO CHRIST
ON HIS CRUCIFIXION.
HIS RIGHTEOUSNESS WAS POURED INTO US
ON THE DAY OF OUR CONVERSION.
WE ARE COMPLETELY HEALED. WITH THIS NEW BIRTH
EVEN THE CHILD WITHIN CANNOT TAUNT
A BODY, WHO IS SPIRIT, FILLED.
SO, WE CAN LIVE
OUR NEW LIFE DAY BY DAY…
WITH AN INNER PEACE SMILE ON OUR FACE.
WE'VE BEEN WASHED
BY THE BLOOD OF THE LAMB,
RECIPIENTS OF GOD'S
RESTORATION, MERCY AND GRACE!

TAKE AWAY FROM RETREAT

SO, YOU'VE JUST ATTENDED A WOMEN'S SUMMIT!!
WHERE YOU'VE FELT ESPECIALLY CLOSE TO OUR FATHER.
YOU'RE GOING HOME WITH REVVED UP EXCITEMENT. YOUR
FAITH IS RENEWED AND SPIRITUAL CHANGES ARE IN ORDER.
NOW, HOW CAN YOU KEEP DISCOURAGEMENTS
AND EVERY DAY LIFE PRESSURES FROM
DRAINING OFF THAT ENTHUSIASM AND BRINGING YOU DOWN?
YOU'VE EXPERIENCED THAT "SPIRITUAL HIGH".
YOU'VE FELT... YES, IT'S JUST GOD'S PRESENCE HERE,
ON THE MOUNTAIN...
IT SEEMS AS IF NO ONE ELSE IS AROUND.
HOW CAN YOU SAVOR, THE EXPERIENCE...
THAT SPIRITUAL HIGH,
THAT ALLOWED YOU TO MOVE TO NEW SPIRITUAL DEPTHS?
FOR NO ONE CAN FOREVER STAY ON THAT "HIGH."
REALITIES OF LIVING RETURNS TO KNOCK YOU DOWN A STEP.
THE GOAL OF THE SPIRITUAL LIFE AS THE PSALMIST DAVID
SAYS, IS TO "SET THE LORD ALWAYS BEFORE ME."
NOT "I SET THE LORD BEFORE ME" AT THE RETREAT.
THEN ALLOW LIFESTYLES AT HOME
TO TAKE OVER...TO COMPETE.
SO, IT'S IMPORTANT THAT WE LEARN HOW TO TAKE AWAY
WHAT WE'VE LEARNED AND ABIDE
IN IT'S TRUTH FROM DAY TO DAY.
MAKE TIME FOR TRANSITION
THE FIRST STEP BEGINS
BEFORE YOU LEAVE THE FOOT OF THE CROSS.
SIFT THROUGH THESE QUESTIONS
IN THE RETREAT ATMOSPHERE.
WHAT TRUTHS, IDEAS, CERTAINTIES IMPRESSED ME?
WHAT MIGHT GOD HAVE BEEN TRYING TO SAY
WHILE I FELT HIS PRESENCE SO NEAR?
WHEN WILL IT BE MOST DIFFICULT FOR ME TO LIVE WHAT I
HAVE GRASPED AT THIS RETREAT?

WHAT DO I MOST NEED TO TAKE HOME WITH ME?
TO ENABLE ME TO WITHSTAND DEFEAT?
WRITE DOWN YOUR THOUGHTS SO YOU
CAN LOOK THEM OVER ONCE YOU RETURN HOME.
BY THIS YOU'RE SAYING, "THE SUMMIT RETREAT
WAS MORE THAN A NICE EXPERIENCE."
YOU'RE STATING
THAT WHAT YOU GLIMPSED OR UNDERSTOOD
WAS NOT JUST ON LOAN.
IT WAS IMPORTANT ENOUGH TO
TAKE IT AWAY.
BECAUSE SPIRITUAL HIGHS CAN GET ELEVATED TO
AN INAPPROPRIATE LEVEL OUR
GOAL MUST BE TO "SET THE LORD ALWAYS BEFORE US"
AND NOT TO GIVE OPPORTUNITY TO THE DEVIL.
WE NEED TO LET PEAK EXPERIENCES
BLEND INTO OUR WHOLE WAY OF LIFE.
"WHATSOEVER WE DO IN WORD OR DEED, DO ALL IN THE
NAME OF THE LORD JESUS." THAT ALONE WILL SUFFICE.
THEN ALL OF LIFE BECOMES INFUSED WITH A
BIT OF THE GLORY OF GOD BECAUSE YOU HAVE PROCESSED
AND REMEMBERED WHAT OCCURRED AT THIS SUMMIT.
TO MAKE YOU WANT TO ALWAYS DO YOUR BEST.

RECALLING WHAT YOU'VE LEARNED
THERE ARE OBVIOUS REMINDERS SUCH
AS INFO IN YOUR WELCOME PACKETS.
MAKE A BOOKMARK TO JOT DOWN **TAKE AWAY** THOUGHTS.
PLACE IT IN A BOOK YOU FREQUENTLY USE,
YOUR COOKBOOK, NOVEL YOU'RE READING
OR THE BIBLE THAT YOU BROUGHT.
OR YOU CAN COME UP WITH YOUR OWN REMINDERS,
A LEAF PRESSED IN YOUR BIBLE,
A SONG THAT TAKES ON DEEPER MEANING,
A BIBLE VERSE THAT SPEAKS DIFFERENTLY TO YOU
THAN IN ALL OF YOUR FORMER READING.
THEN HONOR THE REMINDER ITSELF
BY **PAUSING** WHEN YOU SEE IT.

OR WHEN THAT PHRASE COMES TO MIND
SAY TO GOD "THANK YOU FOR SPEAKING TO ME,
THANKS FOR THIS NEW PEACE THAT I FIND.
AS I TURN NORMAL THOUGHTS
INTO PRAYERS WITHOUT CEASING
I ADVANCE IN THIS SPIRITUAL CLIMB!
I LEARNED THAT TO PRAY WITHOUT CEASING
IS NOT LIVING A LIFE NON-STOP ON BENDED KNEES.
THE APOSTLE PAUL WHO WROTE THOSE WORDS
WAS A HIGHLY ENERGIZED DOER
WHO TRAVELED ABOUT EXTENSIVELY.
HE LIVED HIS LIFE IN TWO LEVELS: DOING IMPORTANT THINGS
AND WITHIN HIMSELF MAKING SPACE
FOR BACK-AND-FORTH INTERACTION WITH GOD.
ALWAYS GIVING HIM FIRST PLACE.
A SIMPLE WAY TO DO THIS IS TO
TURN YOUR PERPETUAL SELF TALK
INTO A CONTINUAL CONVERSATION
WITH GOD EVEN IN YOUR DAILY WALK.
OR WHEN YOU'RE DRIVING ALONG AND THINK,
"WHY IS THAT ODD LOOKING PERSON
ON THE CORNER OF THIS STREET.?"
SWITCH THAT THOUGHT TO A PRAYER, "PLEASE FATHER
HELP HER FIND HER WAY,
WHAT CAN I DO TO HELP HER GET BACK ON HER FEET?"
BREATH PRAYERS
TAKE WHAT YOU LEARNED AT THIS SUMMIT
AND FORM A **"BREATH PRAYER."**

**EVERY NEW DAY IS A BLESSING FROM ABOVE.
ONE WITH ITS OWN POTENTIAL
AND OUTPOURING OF GOD'S LOVE.
SO, CHERISH THIS DAY TO ITS FULLNESS.
LOVE, LAUGH, HOPE AND SING.
LOOKING FORWARD TO YOUR TOMORROWS
FOR NEW CHALLENGES THEY WILL BRING!**

COMFORT ZONE
IS GOD PROMPTING YOU TO DO SOMETHING
THAT IS OUTSIDE OF YOUR "COMFORT ZONE'?
REQUIRING YOU TO FULLY TRUST
THAT... WHEN IN OBEDIENCE TO HIM...
YOU ARE NOT STEPPING OUT ON YOUR OWN?
ARE YOU CONSCIOUS OF OTHERS AROUND YOU...
THE QUIZZICAL LOOK ON THEIR FACE...
QUESTIONING YOUR ACTIONS...AS TO WHETHER
YOU'RE OUT OF LINE, IN SOMEONE ELSE'S SPACE?
DOES THE HOLY SPIRIT GUIDE YOU
TO ADVANCE IN BOLD FAITH...
AFTER YOU'VE ACCEPTED CHRIST AND STUDIED HIS WORD
TO EMBOLDEN YOU FOR LIFE'S RACE?
IT'S TIME TO STOP QUESTIONING
THE FATHER'S WILL AND PURPOSE FOR YOUR LIFE...
TIME TO BUCK UP...IN OBEDIENCE...
TO AVOID CONFLICT AND STRIFE.
TIME TO EMBRACE NOT ONLY THE POWER
BUT THE VERY PRESENCE OF HIM...
WHO GAVE HIS ONLY SON TO
SACRIFICE HIS LIFE FOR OUR SIN.
TIME TO SURRENDER ALL.
ACKNOWLEDGE THE WILL OF OUR CREATOR.
TIME TO STEP OUT IN BOLDNESS
IN FULL TRUST IN OUR DIVINE MAKER.
GOD'S WORD SAYS, HE WHO HAS BEGUN A GOOD WORK IN US
WILL COMPLETE UNTIL THE RETURN OF OUR LORD. DON'T
LOOK FOR ACKNOWLEDGEMENT AND PRAISE FROM MEN...
JUST ENJOY EARTHLY PROVISIONS AND THEN HEAVENLY
REWARD. REVIVE US AGAIN, OH FATHER, FILL EACH HEART
WITH THY LOVE. MAY OUR SOULS BE REKINDLED WITH FIRE
FROM ABOVE. REKINDLE OUR DESIRE TO WALK IN YOUR
SPIRIT. REKINDLE OUR DETERMINATION
TO BE OBEDIENT TO YOUR WILL.REKINDLE,
OH FATHER, THE MANIFESTATIONS OF YOUR GIFTS.
AS WE ALLOW DAILY...YOUR HOLY SPIRIT'S FILL....
SO THAT WHEN WE HAVE PROMPTINGS
THAT ARE OUTSIDE OF OUR COMFORT ZONE.
WE WILL COMPLETELY TRUST IN YOU
ASSURED WE'RE NOT STEPPING OUT ...ON OUR OWN.

CONFESSION

IT HAS BEEN SAID THAT CONFESSION IS GOOD FOR THE SOUL
BUT... UNLESS YOUR CONFESSION IS OF FAITH AND BELIEF
IN JESUS AS SAVIOR, CONFESSION DOES NOT MAKE YOU
WHOLE. YES, WE CAN TALK IN CONFIDENCE WITH OTHERS
ABOUT QUESTIONABLE THINGS WE HAVE DONE...
HOW WE'RE SO SORRY FOR OFFENSES. DECLARING
A NEW, REFORMED, RACE WE HAVE BEGUN.
BUT...UNLESS WE CRY OUT TO GOD, OUR FATHER,
RULER OF EARTH, SKY AND SEA...BELIEVING IN THE BIRTH,
LIFE, DEATH, RESURRECTION AND ASCENSION OF JESUS
OUR SOUL IS NOT COMPLETELY FREE.
SPIRITUAL FREEDOM WITH INNER PEACE COMES ONLY WHEN
WE CONFESS WITH OUR MOUTH OUR BELIEF IN HIM AND
BELIEVE IN OUR HEART THAT HE DIED AND AROSE FOR OUR
SIN. A MERE CONFESSION DOES NOTHING
FOR OUR SOUL. NOR DOES IT PLACE OUR NAME ON GOD'S
ROLL. SO AS A LIFETIME DECLARATION
WHY NOT REACH OUT TO FRIENDS, FAMILY
AND TO THOSE WHOM YOU DO NOT KNOW...
TO TELL THEM ABOUT OUR LIVING SAVIOR. THEN
DIRECT THEM TO GOD'S WORD FOR SPIRITUAL GROWTH.
IN ESSENCE, YES, CONFESSION WILL BE GOOD FOR THE
SOUL. YOUR NAME WRITTEN IN BOLD LETTERS ON GOD'S
ROLL. GIVE YOUR LIFE TO JESUS
WHO ALREADY KNOWS YOUR NAME.
IN RETURN YOU WILL RECEIVE FORGIVENESS, RESTORATION,
INNER PEACE, DIRECTION. YOUR LIFE WILL NEVER BE THE
SAME. AS WE YEARLY CELEBRATE JESUS BIRTH IN A MANGER
LET'S SUBMIT MORE FULLY IN OUR STYLE OF LIVING
TO MIMIC HIS EARTHLY BEHAVIOR.
HE NOW SITS ON THE RIGHT HAND OF GOD THE FATHER
MAKING INTERCESSION FOR US!
THIS DAY...ANY SEASON...
MAKE HIM LORD OF YOUR LIFE...
REMEMBER FORGIVENESS IS NOT AN OPTION
GOD REQUIRES THAT OF US.
BECAUSE IN TRUTH...
HE IS THE ONLY ONE WE CAN REALLY TRUST!

A DECLARATION OF FAITH...

FATHER, YOUR WORD SAYS THAT
YOU ALONE ARE MY STRENGTH.
THOUGH MY STEPS MAY FALTER NOW
YOUR MERCY AND GRACE HAVE NO LENGTH.
A SUREFOOTED DEER CAN CLIMB
EVEN ROCK CLIFFS WITHOUT A SLIP OR SLIDE.
SO, ROCK OF AGES...CLEFT FOR ME.
IN THEE MY SOUL...I WILL HIDE.
YOUR WORD SAYS YOU WILL BRING ME
EVEN OVER MOUNTAINS SAFELY.
MOUNTAINS OF SURGERY, RECUPERATION,
TO RELAXATION...
WHAT AN ASSURING PROMISE TO ME!
SO, I GO TO YOUR WORD, FATHER...
LOOKING FORWARD TO THE MANIFESTATION
OF ALL THE PROMISES THAT APPLY
TO ME NOW AND TO THE NEXT GENERATION.
I DECLARE NOW THAT...
I WILL BE STRONG IN YOUR STRENGTH!
I WILL BE SUREFOOTED AS A DEER!
I WILL TRAVEL SAFELY OVER THIS MOUNTAIN!
I WILL PROCEED WITHOUT FEAR!!
TO GOD BE THE GLORY
AMEN...AMEN

Habakkuk 3:19 TLB

**"THE SOVEREIGN LORD
IS MY STRENGTH.
HE WILL MAKE ME AS
SUREFOOTED
AS A DEER
AND BRING ME
SAFELY...
OVER THE MOUNTAINS."**

LOOK TO THE SON

LET US SOAR LIKE THE EAGLE!
NOT RUN WITH TURKEYS WHO FLY LOW.
LET US SEEK THE HOLY SPIRIT'S GUIDANCE
AS TO WHICH DIRECTION WE SHOULD GO.
AS THE EAGLE LOOKS TOWARD THE SUN
FOR STRENGTH FOR THE STIRVE,
SO ALSO, WE MUST "KNOW" THE "SON."
TO SUSTAIN US THROUGH THIS LIFE.
DO YOU BELIEVE HE WAS CROSS CRUCIFIED,
DIED AND AROSE FROM THE GRAVE?
HAVE YOU ASKED HIM
FOR FORGIVENESS, INVITED CHRIST IN.
DETERMINED TO TURN FROM YOUR SIN?
THEN, MY FRIEND, THANK GOD YOU ARE SAVED!
BAPTIZED, FOLLOW THE EXAMPLE OF JESUS
AS IS STATED IN GOD'S WORD.
LET OTHERS KNOW OF YOUR ACCEPTANCE OF JESUS
AS YOUR PERSONAL SAVIOR AND LORD.
STUDY GOD'S WORD.
IF YOU LACK WISDOM, JUST ASK.
YOU'LL RECEIVE UNDERSTANDING
FOR COMPLETION OF LIFE'S TASKS.
ONLY THEN CAN YOU SOAR LIKE THE EAGLE
INSTEAD OF
RUNNING WITH TURKEYS WHO FLY LOW,
AS THE HOLY SPIRIT DIVINELY GUARDS
AND GIVES DIRECTIONS AS YOU GO.

PROVERBS 3:5
TRUST IN THE LORD WITH ALL OF YOUR HEART,
LEAN NOT TO YOUR OWN UNDERSTANDING.
IN ALL THY WAYS ACKNOWLEDGE HIM
AND HE WILL DIRECT YOUR PATH.

PERSONAL RESPONSIBILITY

HEAVENLY FATHER,
YOU'VE SHOWN TO ME
THAT ALLOWING
THE HOLY SPIRIT TO DIRECT
IS A PERSONAL RESPONSIBILITY.
OTHERS CAN PRAY SINGULARLY OR IN MASS
FOR THE STRENGTH THEY THINK
IS NECESSARY FOR SOMEONE ELSE'S TASK.
BUT UNLESS HUMBLE SUBMISSION ....
IS PERSONALLY UNDERTAKEN
THOSE PRAYERS WON'T BE ANSWERED
ALTHOUGH WE'RE STILL NEVER FORSAKEN.
FOR WHEN YOU CREATED US ...
YOU
GAVE
EACH ONE A
CHOICE.
YOU WILL NOT OVERRIDE OUR WILL
IF WE DON'T LISTEN TO YOUR VOICE.
WE NEED NOT BE DISMAYED
AT THE CONSEQUENCES
OF OTHER'S VAIN PRIDE.
GOD MAKES THE DECISIONS...
HE ALONE. KNOWS WHAT IS INSIDE.
SO, THANK YOU, FATHER
FOR REINFORCING THAT REVELATION.
AS IT APPLIES TO ALL.
WHO HAVE ACCEPTED SALVATION.
NOW THERE'S NO NEED TO CRY
NO NEED TO CONTINUE TO FRET.
FOR WHEN FOLLOWING
GOD'S DIRECTION.
NO ONE
HAS BEEN...FAILED...YET.

THERE IS A BLESSING

THE SONG SAYS, I'M GOING THROUGH
YES, I'M GOING THROUGH,
I'LL PAY THE PRICE
WHATEVER OTHERS DO.
I'LL TAKE THE WAY WITH
THE LORD'S DESPISED FEW.
I'VE STARTED WITH JESUS
AND I'M GOING THROUGH.
THERE IS A BLESSING
ON THE OTHER SIDE OF THROUGH.
GOD HAS ALREADY PROMISED
HIS JOY WILL BE STRENGTH FOR YOU.
HE WILL NEVER LEAVE YOU ALL ALONE
SINCE FOR ALL OF OUR SINS
HE ALREADY ATONED.
FRET NOT, MY FRIEND, FRET NOT,
FOR THERE IS A BLESSING
ON THE OTHER SIDE OF THROUGH.
BE PATIENT...FOR PATIENCE IS ONLY
A COURAGEOUS PERSEVERANCE.
ENHANCED AND EMPOWERED
BY GOD'S BLESSED ASSURANCE.
OH YES...THERE IS A BLESSING
ON THE OTHER SIDE OF THROUGH...
TRUST GOD, BELIEVE, RECEIVE, PRAISE GOD
BECAUSE HE IS USING YOU.
YOU'VE STARTED WITH JESUS...
SO NOW KEEP GOING THROUGH!

TRUSTING CHRIST TODAY

FOR THOSE
WHO ARE
TRUSTING CHRIST TODAY...
THERE IS
HOPE.
JUST
GO TO THE WORD OF GOD
TO BROADEN
YOUR SPIRITUAL SCOPE.
WHETHER YOU ARE
BASKING IN BLESSINGS
OR GRINDING THROUGH ILLNESS,
AGING OR GRIEF...
THERE IS HOPE IN CHRIST
AND
PROGRESSIVE RELIEF.
GOD'S WORD SAYS...IN THE FIRST CHAPTER OF PETER
**"PRAISE BE TO THE GOD AND FATHER OF OUR LORD JESUS
CHRIST! IN HIS GREAT MERCY HE HAS GIVEN US NEW BIRTH
INTO A LIVING HOPE THROUGH
THE RESURRECTION OF JESUS
CHRIST FROM THE DEAD, AND INTO AN INHERITANCE THAT
CAN NEVER PERISH, SPOIL OR FADE. THIS INHERITANCE IS
KEPT IN HEAVEN FOR YOU, WHO THROUGH FAITH ARE
SHIELDED BY GOD'S POWER UNTIL THE COMING OF THE
SALVATION THAT IS READY TO BE REVEALED IN THE LAST
TIME. IN ALL THIS YOU GREATLY REJOICE, THOUGH NOW FOR
A LITTLE WHILE YOU MAY HAVE HAD TO SUFFER GRIEF AND
ALL KINDS OF TRIALS. THESE HAVE COME SO THAT THE
PROVEN GENUINENESS OF YOUR FAITH...OF GREATER
WORTH THAN GOLD, WHICH PERISHES EVEN THOUGH
REFINED BY FIRE...MAY RESULT IN PRAISE, GLORY AND
HONOR WHEN JESUS CHRIST IS REVEALED**

IN GOD, THROUGH CHRIST, WE HAVE DEVELOPED A TRUST.
BECAUSE GOD RAISED CHRIST FROM THE DEAD,
BELIEF IN HIM IS A MUST.
OUR HOPE CAN BE PLACED CONFIDENTLY
IN HIM BECAUSE GOD GAVE HIM GLORY.
TRUST, OBEDIENCE, FAITH... ENHANCES OUR LIFE STORY.
THE NEW LIFE HE GAVE TO US WILL LAST FOREVER.
WHAT CHRIST DID FOR US ON THE CROSS
NO MAN CAN SEVER.
PEOPLE ARE LIKE GRASS THAT QUICKLY DIES AWAY.
THE WORD OF GOD IS ETERNAL AND GIVEN FREELY...
NO PRICE LEFT FOR US TO PAY.
BECAUSE WE HAVE BELIEVED
AND RECEIVED JESUS AS OUR PERSONAL SAVIOR
HE CLEANSED US AND GAVE THE HOLY SPIRIT TO HELP US
CHANGE BEHAVIOR.
SO, NO MATTER WHAT
WE CAN HAVE LOVE FOR ALL SISTERS AND BROTHERS.
WE ALSO HAVE AN INNER PEACE
WHICH SURPASSES ANY OTHER.
MY FRIEND, IF YOU ARE BASKING IN BLESSINGS
OR GRINDING THROUGH ILLNESS OR GRIEF.
PSALM 46:10 "BE STILL AND KNOW"
AS YOU
MEDITATE ON GOD'S WORD
YOU WILL REALIZE
THE HOPE IN HIM
AND EXPERIENCE
PROGRESSIVE RELIEF.

FREE INDEED

SINCE GOD SET YOU FREE YOU ARE FREE INDEED.
WHETHER FROM A PAINFUL EXPERIENCE
OR ADVICE THAT YOU DID NOT HEED.
PEACE SWEPT GENTLY OVER YOUR MIND
AND THROUGH YOUR SOUL.
A REMINDER THAT YOU ARE A PROMISE RECIPIENT
SINCE YOUR NAME IS ON HIS ROLL.
YOU NO LONGER DWELL
ON DARK MEMORIES SATAN BRINGS TO MIND
BECAUSE GOD HAS GIVEN YOU AUTHORITY
TO PLACE SATAN NOT FORWARD BUT BEHIND.
SO, HE CAN NO LONGER TAKE YOU PLACES
WHERE YOU HAVE NO DESIRE TO BE.
JUST DECLARE TO HIM AND YOURSELF
THAT YOU ARE DEAD TO HIM AND THE WORLD...
FOR BY THE BLOOD OF JESUS YOU HAVE BEEN SET FREE!
NO MORE MOANING AND LONGING
FOR THINGS FROM THE PAST.
YOU ARE NOW STEADFAST, UNMOVABLE,
PRESSING FORWARD IN THE KNOWLEDGE...
"ONLY WHAT IS DONE FOR CHRIST WILL LAST."
YOUR NEW MANTRA, FREE, FREE, PRAISE GOD I AM FREE...
WITH UNWAVERING FAITH
AND TRUST IN GOD'S FUTURE FOR ME"!

SONG BECAUSE OF CHRIST

I'M IN GOOD SHAPE FOR THE SHAPE I'M IN
BECAUSE OF CHRIST.
I AM IN GOOD SHAPE FOR THE SHAPE
I'M IN BECAUSE OF CHRIST.
HE STRENGTHENED MY BODY,
MY MIND RENEWED,
NOW I'M WALKING TOWARDS HEAVEN
WITH A DIFFERENT VIEW
I'M IN GOOD SHAPE FOR THE SHAPE I'M IN
BECAUSE OF CHRIST.

YOU'RE IN GOOD SHAPE FOR THE SHAPE YOU'RE IN
BECAUSE OF CHRIST.
YOU ARE IN GOOD SHAPE FOR THE SHAPE YOU'RE IN
BECAUSE OF CHRIST.
HE STRENGTHENED YOUR BODY,
YOUR MIND RENEWED,
NOW YOU'RE WALKING TOWARD HEAVEN
WITH A DIFFERENT VIEW.
YOU'RE IN GOOD SHAPE FOR THE SHAPE
YOU'RE IN BECAUSE OF CHRIST.

STILL SINGING HIS PRAISES
IN THE SHAPE I'M IN
BECAUSE OF CHRIST.
I'M STILL SINGING HIS PRAISES
IN THE SHAPE I'M IN
BECAUSE OF CHRIST.
HE STRENGTHENED MY BODY,
MY MIND RENEWED
NOW I'M WALKING TOWARD HEAVEN
WITH A DIFFERENT VIEW.
STILL SINGING HIS PRAISES
IN THE SHAPE I'M IN
BECAUSE OF CHRIST.

BEST NOT GOOD ENOUGH

WHEN YOUR BEST IS NEVER
QUITE GOOD ENOUGH
AND THE RULES OF THE GAME
SEEMINGLY MAKE LIFE TOO TOUGH...
TO YOUR SECRET CLOSET OF PRAYER
YOU MUST QUIETLY GO
TO CONVERSE WITH OUR "FATHER'
WHO STILL LOVES US SO,.
IN SPITE OF UNGODLY THOUGHTS AND OUR
INTENTIONS TO EXPRESS
HE SILENCES AN UNRULY TONGUE
FOR HE KNOWS FOR US...THAT IS BEST.
I'M SO GRATEFUL OUR HEAVENLY FATHER
WILL REMAIN IN CONTROL.
IN LIFE'S DEMEANING SITUATIONS
HE WILL HEAL...AND MAKE WHOLE.
WE REALIZE THAT WE
ARE ESPECIALLY LOVED
BY A GOD OF COMPASSION
WHO IS ALWAYS MOVED...
WHENEVER WE CLAIM HIM AS
PERSONAL SAVIOR AND LORD.
ALLOWING HIM TO SPEAK GENTLY THROUGH
DAILY READING OF HIS WORD.
BE ENCOURAGED...MY FRIEND
THIS LONG... LONG NIGHT WILL PASS.

THE NEW HAPPINESS YOU WILL FIND
WILL BE ONE THAT WILL LAST.
ACCEPT THE COMFORTER...
HURTS WILL BEGIN TO FADE.

YOU'LL LOOK BACK IN AMAZEMENT
AT THE PROGRESS YOU HAVE MADE!

ACCEPT...

ON THE MOUNTAIN WE FEEL REVIVED...
ENJOYING PRAYER AND PRAISE
FEELING EXTREMELY ALIVE!
BUT IT'S IN THE VALLEY THAT WE SEEM TO GROW
STILL FEELING THE PRESENCE OF OUR GOD
WHO LOVES US SO.
IN THE VALLEY WE SEE OURSELVES IN RETROSPECT.
THE PART OF OURSELVES WE ACCEPT
AND OTHER PARTS WE NEED TO REJECT.
ACCEPT
THAT PART THAT GIVES YOU A DEEPER LOVE
FOR ALL SISTERS AND BROTHERS,
PREDESTINED RELATIONSHIPS BY OUR FATHER ABOVE.
THE PART THAT GIVES YOU A GUT LEVEL APPRECIATION
FOR THE POSITIVE PART OTHERS HAVE
PLAYED IN VARIOUS SITUATIONS.
ACCEPT
YOUR ZEAL TO STUDY GOD'S WORD...
ENHANCING YOUR DAYS AS
YOU WALK HUMBLY WITH OUR LORD.
ACCEPT
THE HOLY SPIRIT'S GUIDANCE IN PICKING YOUR BATTLES
EVER AWARE OF THE "ONE" IN CHARGE
WHO KEEPS YOU FROM GETTING
OUTRAGEOUS AND RATTLED.
WHEN LIFE PRESENTS AS
CHALLENGE AFTER CHALLENGE
THREATENING YOUR DETERMINATION TO "STAND STILL"
AND STEADY...NEVER LOSING YOUR BALANCE.
ACCEPT
ALL THE PROMISES GOD'S WORD PRESENTS TO YOU & ME...
TO WALK WITH US HERE ON EARTH
THEN SEND ANGELS
TO GUIDE US INTO ETERNITY.

SELF CHECK TEST (READ JONAH 3 & 4)

IF YOU'VE BEEN WOUNDED AND BATTERED BEYOND WHAT
WORDS CAN EXPRESS. THEN JUST SIT AND RELAX
A MOMENT WHILE TAKING THIS SELF CHECK TEST.
GOD'S WORD SAYS WE MUST FORGIVE
IN ORDER FOR HIM TO FORGIVE US.
HE OWES US NO EXPLANATIONS.
WE OWE HIM OUR LOVE AND TRUST.

1. FIRST QUESTION, **HAVE YOU FORGIVEN YOURSELF AND
OTHERS? IF SO, JUST READ THE REST** IF NOT,
YOU'RE A LIKELY CANDIDATE TO BENEFIT FROM THIS TEST
OLD JONAH SPENT TIME IN THE BELLY OF A GREAT FISH
BECAUSE HE CHOSE NOT TO GO TO NINEVEH.
HE CHOSE NOT TO WITNESS.

**2. HAVE YOU CHOSEN A PATH
THAT'S NOT PLEASING TO THE LORD?
3. ARE YOU JEOPARDIZING YOUR SOUL'S STATUS BY NOT
SHARING GOD'S WORD?**
AFTER JONAH WAS EJECTED NEAR THE LAND
WHERE HE HAD BEEN SENT.
HE DECIDED TO OBEY GOD...TO TEACH OTHERS TO REPENT.

**4. HAVE YOU RELUCTANTLY CHOSEN TO TELL OTHERS
ABOUT SALVATION? 5 .WHEN THEY'VE ACCEPTED CHRIST
IS YOUR HEART SHORT ON ELATION?**
THE COUNTRY OF NINEVEH TURNED TO GOD AND THE
RESPONSE WAS JOY AND GLADNESS.
BUT JONAH FELT BECAUSE OF HIS PERSONAL HURT BY THEM.
(THEY WERE IN FACT
RESPONSIBLE FOR HIS OWN MOTHER'S DEATH)
THEY DID NOT DESERVE FORGIVENESS...
HE WAS FILLED WITH A DEEP SADNESS.
SO, HE WENT UP ON A HILL
ABOVE THE CITY TO SULK AND TO POUT.
BECAUSE GOD TURNED FROM PUNISHING NINEVEH AS THEY
ACCEPTED HIM WITH A SHOUT.

**6. ARE YOU POUTING AND SULKING BECAUSE OF CERTAIN
ONES GOD CHOSE TO FORGIVE?
7. EVEN AFTER YOUR EARNEST PRAYERS ARE YOU REALLY
GLAD THAT AS CHRISTIANS THEY CAN NOW LIVE?**

8. DO YOU RESENT THE FACT THAT AFTER THEY HAVE
WOUNDED YOU SO DEEPLY
GOD STILL ANSWERED PRAYERS ON THEIR BEHALF
AND FORGAVE THEIR SINS COMPLETELY
SO NOW
THEY CAN LOOK YOU
STRAIGHT IN THE EYE WITH A GENUINE SMILE SO SWEETLY?
9. WOULD YOU, LIKE JONAH,
RATHER SEE THEIR COMPLETE DEMISE...
SOME SUFFERING, HARD TIMES, AND BRINY,
TEARS BURNING THEIR EYES?
GOD WAS STILL MERCIFUL TO JONAH AS ON THAT HILL TOP
HE JUST SAT IN THE HEAT. HE CAUSED GOURD BRANCHES TO
GROW OVER HIS SHELTER,
SHADING HIM FROM HEAT FROM HIS HEAD TO HIS FEET.
10. HAVE YOU RECOGNIZED AND GIVEN
THANKS FOR THE SHADE GOD HAS PROVIDED FOR YOU?
11. DO YOU THANK HIM FOR MERCY AND GRACE HE
BESTOWED THAT BROUGHT YOU SAFELY THROUGH?
THERE WAS ANOTHER LESSON THAT GOD SAW A NEED TO
TEACH. SO, HE CREATED A WORM TO DESTROY THE SHADE
THAT HAD SHELTERED JONAH FROM THE HEAT.
THEN JONAH WAS OUTRAGED THAT GOD SEEMED TO HAVE
CHANGED HIS MIND ABOUT SHADING HIM FROM THE HEAT.
NOW NO COMFORT OR PEACE COULD HE FIND. THE LESSON
BEING TAUGHT WAS TO SHOW JONAH THAT GOD HAD A RIGHT
TO SAVE NINEVEH'S SOULS. THAT GOD ALONE HAD THE
AUTHORITY OVER WHOSE NAME
APPEARS ON ETERNITY'S ROLL.
HE ALONE CREATED US AND PUT US IN CHARGE OF THE
LAND. HE ALONE DECIDES WHO ENTERS HEAVEN ALSO WHO
WILL BE BANNED. 12. DO YOU FEEL BETRAYED WHEN GOD
SHOWS MERCY ON OTHERS ALLOWING THEM TO PROSPER
AS CHRISTIAN SISTERS AND BROTHERS? THE LAST QUESTION
ON THIS TEST....IF YOU THINK ABOUT IT JUST MIGHT BLOW
YOUR MIND13. IF WE SHOW NO MERCY TO OTHERS, HOW
MUCH MERCY, GRACE, OR PEACE WILL WE FIND?
14. WELL FRIENDS...DID WE GET THE POINT?
15. DID ANY OF THESE WORDS HIT HOME FOR US?
IF SO, ASK GOD TO FORGIVE AND SHOW MERCY AS WE
DETERMINE TO OBEY HIM...AND TRUST.

THANKFUL ATTITUDE

MY DEVOTIONAL READING FOR TODAY SAYS
WINDOWS OF HEAVEN ARE OPENED
BY A THANKFUL ATTITUDE.
AS LOOKING UP WITH A GRATEFUL HEART
WILL GLIMPSE GLORY FOR YOU!
YOU CANNOT YET LIVE IN HEAVEN BUT
YOUR EXPERIENCE GLIMPSES REVIVE HOPE.

BROADENING WIDELY
YOUR PRESENT SPIRITUAL SCOPE.

THANKFULNESS IS NOT A MAGIC FORMULA.
IT IS THE LANGUAGE OF LOVE...
TRANSPORTED BY THE HOLY SPIRIT
TO OUR SOVEREIGN GOD ABOVE.

IT ALLOWS US TO REJOICE IN OUR FATHER
IN THE MIDST OF SORROW, TRIALS, TRIBULATIONS...
ENHANCES THE JOY OF THE LORD
AS OUR STRENGTH IN EVERY SITUATION.

SO, LET'S LIVE TODAY WITH
A RENEWED ATTITUDE OF GRATEFULLNESS.
STRIVING TO WALK THE UPWARD WAY
WHILE EXPERIENCING GOD'S GRACE...IN THE PRESS.

ENCOURAGING DAILY PRAYER DURING RECUPERATION

HEAVENLY FATHER,
PLEASE DO NOT LET ME TAKE FOR GRANTED
WHAT YOU, IN YOUR MERCY, HAVE DONE FOR ME.
FOR I HAVE A POSITIVE HISTORY OF MIRACULOUS HEALING
AND YOU CONTINUE TO KEEP ME DISEASE FREE.
THERE IS NO HABIT THAT CANNOT BE RELEASED TO YOU.
AS I'VE ALREADY CLAIMED YOU
AS MY LORD AND SAVIOR.
WHEN I ACCEPTED YOU INTO MY HEART,
YOU GAVE ME YOUR HOLY SPIRIT TO EMPOWER ME
TO CHANGE MY BEHAVIOR.
HEAVENLY FATHER, PLEASE GIVE ME A DESIRE TO DO MORE
TO READ, TO STUDY YOUR WORD
AND ON YOU DEPEND.
FOR I WANT TO BE OBEDIENT RIGHT THROUGH MY VERY END.
I'VE BEEN TOLD, SCRIPTURE SAYS, DO NOT FORSAKE THE
ASSEMBLING OF YOUR SELVES TOGETHER.
THAT MEANS PRAYER AND PRAISE IN GOD'S HOUSE
AFTER THE PANDEMIC REGARDLESS OF THE WEATHER.
HELP ME TO WANT TO TAKE PART IN BIBLE STUDY.
TO REINFORCE AND INFORM ME OF THE
TOTAL AWESOMENESS OF YOUR POWER.
THEN AS I GROW
IN THE KNOWLEDGE OF CHRIST,
HELP MY LEVEL OF COMMITMENT TO INCREASE.
AND EXPERIENCES BE ENHANCED WITH INNER PEACE.
BECAUSE FATHER, OF MY LOVE FOR YOU AND THAT
YOU FIRST LOVED ME,
AND LED ME TO REPENT.
WITH THIS TRUE REPENTANCE
ENHANCE MY NATURAL DESIRE
TO BE TOTOTALLY OBEDIENT, LORD.
HEAVENLY FATHER,
I DO NOT TAKE FOR GRANTED
WHAT YOU HAVE ALREADY DONE FOR ME.
PLEASE LET MY POSITIVE LIFESTYLE REFLECT
THAT YOUR WORD HAS SET ME FREE.

JUST LET THE WHISPER OF THE NAME OF YOUR SON, JESUS
BRING FORTH YOUR POWER TO RESIST ANY HABIT THAT
DAMAGES MY PHYSICAL OR MENTAL HEALTH
OR IN FACT, DAMAGES MY WITNESS TO MY FAMILY.
EVEN DIRECT ME SOMETIMES AS I SURF THROUGH CHANNELS
TO STOP TO LISTEN TO TEACHERS AND PREACHERS...
TO PRAY WITH THEM, SING WITH THEM, PRAISE WITH THEM,
TO FEED MY SOUL AS YOUR WORD TEACHES.
FATHER, WHILE I AM ALONE, RECUPERATING YES, JUST
ALONE RECUPERATING IN MY QUIET PLACE
I WANT TO FEEL YOUR PRESENCE CLOSE TO ME AS IN MY LIFE
I GIVE YOU, YOUR DESERVED SPACE. AMEN

(INSPIRED BY A GOSPEL MESSAGE)

GOD SAYS "LEAVE IT ALONE"

WE SHALL NOT WALK IN FEAR!
GOD SAYS, LEAVE IT ALONE.
YOU ARE MY PRECIOUS CHILD.
YOU ARE NEVER ON YOUR OWN.

ACCEPT MY INNER PEACE
DO NOT TRY TO UNDERSTAND
WHEN AT TIMES, TROUBLES SEEM NOT TO CEASE.

HE REMAINS IN SUPREME CONTROL
OVER ALL OF LIFE'S CIRCUMSTANCE.
FOR EACH AND EVERY SITUATION GOD ALREADY HAS A PLAN.

SO, HE SAYS, MY CHILD, "LEAVE IT ALONE".
STAND STILL, ACKNOWLEDGE ME,
WHO FOR YOUR SINS ALREADY ATONED.

BE STILL AND KNOW THAT I AM GOD.
I SETTLED IT ALL LONG AGO.

SO, TRUST ME! "LEAVE IT ALONE"
STUDY MY WORD, HAVE UNWAIVERING FAITH
AND IN IT'S PRECEPTS AND OBEDIENCE...GROW!

ENCOURAGING PERSONAL WITNESSING

QUESTIONS & ANSWERS
A PLEA FROM...A NEIGHBOR, A FRIEND, A WOULD-BE FRIEND...
WAITING FOR A SPIRITUAL RESCUE. IS IT YOUR ASSIGNMENT?

QUESTIONS?
SOMEBODY, ANYBODY.
WOULD YOU SHARE GOD'S LOVE WITH ME?
RIGHT WHERE I AM NOW?
BROKEN DOWN, DEFEATED, DISILLUSIONED
WITH A FROWN SEEMINGLY EMBEDDED IN MY BROW?
I MIGHT BE SITTING RIGHT BESIDE YOU
WITH WINDS OF DOUBT AND LACK OF KNOWLEDGE
RAGING ALL AROUND...
NOT AN INKLING OF WHERE I AM
OR WHERE I MIGHT BE BOUND.
IS THERE A WORD OF ENCOURAGEMENT, ENLIGHTENMENT,
INSPIRATION SOMEWHERE?
IS THERE A POSITIVE WAY OUT
THAT SOMEBODY, ANYBODY WILL BE WILLING TO SHARE?
MY WORLD IS EMPTY, FRIENDS AND FAMILY FEW.
COULD MY SPIRITUAL "PICK ME UP" ...   MY SPIRITUAL "HIGH"
MY WORD OF SALVATION BE ASSIGNED BY GOD TO YOU?
DON'T MISS YOUR OPPORTUNITY...
SOMEBODY, ANYBODY, IS MY RESCUE ON THE WAY?
OR MUST I JUST DROWN IN THIS RIVER OF NOTHINGNESS?
CAN I BE SAVED.... TODAY?

ANSWERS

WE HAVE A CHOICE **ISAIAH 1:18 TLB "COME, LET'S TALK THIS OVER SAYS THE LORD; NO MATTER HOW DEEP THE STAIN OF YOUR SINS, I CAN TAKE IT OUT AND MAKE YOU AS CLEAN AS FRESHLY FALLEN SNOW. EVEN IF YOU ARE STAINED AS RED AS CRIMSON, I CAN MAKE**
YOU WHITE AS WOOL!

ROMANS 3:23 TLB "ALL HAVE SINNED AND COME
SHORT OF THE GLORY OF GOD"

JOHN 3:16 TLB "GOD SO LOVED THE WORLD THAT HE GAVE HIS ONLY BEGOTTEN SON SO THAT ANYONE WHO BELIEVES IN HIM SHALL NOT PERISH BUT HAVE ETERNAL LIFE"

ACTS 16: 30B-31B TLB "WHAT MUST I DO TO BE SAVED? "BELIEVE ON THE LORD JESUS AND YOU WILL BE SAVED AND ALL OF YOUR HOUSEHOLD."

ROMANS 10:9-10 TLB "FOR IT IS BY BELIEVING IN HIS HEART THAT A MAN BECOMES RIGHT WITH GOD; AND WITH HIS MOUTH HE TELLS OTHERS OF HIS FAITH, CONFIRMING HIS SALVATION."

EPHESIANS 2:8-9-10A TLB "BECAUSE OF HIS KINDNESS YOU HAVE BEEN SAVED THROUGH TRUSTING IN CHRIST. AND EVEN TRUSTING IS NOT OF YOURSELVES; IT TOO IS A GIFT FROM GOD. SALVATION IS NOT A REWARD FOR THE GOOD WE HAVE DONE, SO NONE OF US CAN TAKE ANY CREDIT FOR IT. IT IS GOD HIMSELF WHO HAS MADE US WHAT WE ARE AND GIVEN US NEW LIVES FROM CHRIST JESUS."

HEBREWS 9:12TLB THE BLOOD OF CHRIST
ALREADY PAID THE PRICE ONCE FOR ALL!

REVELATION 3:20- TLB
LOOK! I HAVE BEEN STANDING AT THE DOOR AND I AM CONSTANTLY KNOCKING.
IF ANYONE HEARS ME CALLING HIM
AND OPENS THE DOOR,
I WILL COME IN
AND FELLOWSHIP WITH HIM
AND HE WITH ME."

ROMANS 5:6-11 TLB

"WHEN WE WERE UTTERLY HELPLESS WITH NO WAY OF
ESCAPE, CHRIST CAME AT JUST THE RIGHT TIME AND DIED
FOR US SINNERS WHO HAD NO USE FOR HIM. EVEN IF WE
WERE GOOD, WE REALLY WOULDN'T EXPECT ANYONE TO DIE
FOR US, THOUGH, OF COURSE THAT MIGHT BE BARELY
POSSIBLE. BUT GOD SHOWED HIS GREAT LOVE FOR US BY
SENDING CHRIST TO DIE FOR US WHILE WERE STILL SINNERS.
AND SINCE BY HIS BLOOD HE DID ALL THIS FOR US AS
SINNERS, HOW MUCH MORE WILL HE DO FOR US NOW THAT
HE HAS DECLARED US NOT GUILTY? NOW HE WILL SAVE US
FROM ALL OF GOD'S WRATH TO COME.
AND SINCE, WHEN WE WERE HIS
ENEMIES, WE WERE BROUGHT BACK TO GOD BY THE DEATH
OF HIS SON, WHAT BLESSINGS HE MUST HAVE FOR US NOW
THAT WE ARE HIS FRIEND, AND HE IS LIVING WITHIN US.
NOW WE REOICE IN OUR WONDERFUL NEW
RELATIONSHIP WITH OUR GOD...ALL BECAUSE OF WHAT OUR
LORD JESUS CHRIST HAS DONE IN DYING FOR OUR SINS...
MAKING US FRIENDS OF GOD."
AND THAT'S THE REST OF THE STORY....
SO GLAD YOU ASKED!

"ENCOURAGE YOURSELF" THROUGH PRAISE
SONG OF LOVE AND PRAISE

LET'S SING A SONG TOGETHER.
A SONG OF LOVE AND PRAISE.
LET'S LIFT OUR HANDS UP TO OUR LORD
AS OUR VOICES
WE MELODICALLY RAISE.
OH, HOW YOU LOVE US, O GOD
ENOUGH TO SACRIFICE YOUR ONLY SON.
OUR EYES WE LIFT TO YOU
IN HUMBLE PRAISE
FOR YOUR BLESSINGS,
EACH AND EVERY ONE!
YOU'VE COVERED US WITH PROTECTION
FROM DANGERS BOTH SEEN AND UNSEEN.
YOUR ARMS OF LOVE ENFOLD US
WITH PEACE…
MORE THAN WE HAVE EVER DREAMED.
YOU HAVE SATURATED US WITH
BOTH YOUR MERCY AND YOUR GRACE.
WITH CONSTANT REASSURANCE
OF YOUR GUIDANCE FOR LIFE'S RACE.
SOMETIMES, FATHER,
IT IS HARD IN
OUR SEASON OF LIFE TO BE CONTENT.
HARD TO BELIEVE THAT OUR CIRCUMSTANCES
CAN EVEN BE HEAVEN SENT.
BUT ESPECIALLY IN OUR TRIALS
WE MUST STILL HUMBLY BOW
AND ACCEPT THE JOY AND STRENGTH YOU GIVE
DURING THE DARK TIMES
WHICH YOU ALLOW.
OH, WE CAN STILL SING A SONG TOGETHER!
A SONG OF LOVE,
A SONG OF PRAISE,
A SONG OF TRUST.
TO ACKNOWLEDGE GOD'S FAITHFULNESS
NEVER FAILS.

A SONG OF TRUST.
TO ACKNOWLEDGE GOD'S FAITHFULNESS
NEVER FAILS.
TO ACKNOWLEDGE
OUR GOD WILL TAKE CARE OF US.

WE'VE ACCEPTED YOU AS OUR PRECIOUS LORD AND SAVIOR
WHICH ENTITLED US TO YOUR HOLY SPIRIT'S
EMPOWERMENT TO CHANGE ATTITUDES AND BEHAVIOR
THAT MAY NOT REFLECT YOU AS FATHER OF US ALL
OR DOES NOT GIVE YOU GLORY
FOR PICKING US UP WHEN WE FALL.

BLESS US TO SPEAK POSITIVITY
INTO THOSE THAT WE MEET…
WITH ENCOURAGEMENT
TO ALL THOSE YOU ALLOW US TO GREET.

BLESS US TO WITNESS OF YOU BY OUR LIFESTYLE.

LET US HASTEN TO DO YOUR WILL,

AS THE SONG SAYS
WE MIGHT HAVE "JUST A LITTLE WHILE". AMEN

THEREFORE, SINCE WE ARE SURROUNDED BY SO GREAT A CLOUD OF WITNESSES, LET US ALSO LAY ASIDE EVERY WEIGHT, AND SIN WHICH CLINGS SO CLOSELY, AND LET US RUN WITH ENDURANCE THE RACE THAT IS SET BEFORE US, LOOKING TO JESUS, THE FOUNDER AND PERFECTER OF OUR FAITH, WHO FOR THE JOY THAT WAS SET BEFORE HIM ENDURED THE CROSS, DESPISING THE SHAME, AND IS SEATED AT THE RIGHT HAND OF THE THRONE OF GOD. CONSIDER HIM WHO ENDURED FROM SINNERS SUCH HOSTILITY AGAINST HIMSELF, SO THAT YOU MAY NOT GROW WEARY OR FAINTHEARTED.

MUSINGS

HEAVENLY FATHER, WE THANK YOU!

HEAVENLY FATHER, WE THANK YOU,
FOR THE BEAUTY OF THE GRASS THAT IS STILL SO GREEN,
FOR THE VIVID COLORS OF THE FALLING LEAVES...
FOR BLESSINGS YOU'VE BESTOWED ON US
BOTH SEEN AND UNSEEN.
WE THANK YOU, FOR THE AWESOME SKIES
WHETHER BLUE WITH BILLOWY WHITE CLOUDS OR GREY...
'[FOR THE PASSING OF SUMMER INTO AUTUMN.
FATHER, THANK YOU...AGAIN...TODAY...
FOR FAMILY, FRIENDS AND LOVED ONES TOO.
WE OFFER PRAISE, HONOR AND GLORY...
YES, WE OWE OUR LIVES TO YOU!   AMEN

AFTER AUTUMN

AFTER AUTUMN COMES A NEW WINTER.
WITH CHILLY WINDS TO CLEANSE OUR ATMOSPHERE.
WITH PREDICTED HEAPS OF SLEET, ICE AND SNOW,
BUT WITH GOD ON OUR SIDE...WE FACE IT WITHOUT FEAR.
AS WE KNOW THE FLOWERS AND LIVING THINGS MUST DIE
THEN IN SPRING BE BIRTHED ANEW.
SO ALSO, WHEN WE AS YOUR CHILDREN DIE...
FOR REBIRTH OUR SPIRIT WILL RETURN TO YOU.
THE ONE WHO SENT HIS SON TO SAVE US
THEN DIRECTS US SAFELY THROUGH...
TO BASK IN THE SUNLIGHT OF YOUR SWEET LOVE...
YOUR WONDROUS FACE TO BEHOLD...
TO REUNITE WITH PRECIOUS LOVED ONES
IN A LAND WHERE WE'LL NEVER GROW OLD.
WE LOVE YOU, FATHER
AND IN YOU WE CONTINUE TO TRUST...
SO, FACING ANOTHER LONG WINTER
WILL NOT BE FOREBODING TO US.
EACH DAY BRINGS A BLESSING
AND ALSO, A CHALLENGE WITH IT
TO READ, RELAX,
STIMULATE OUR MIND
AND KEEP OUR BODY PHYSICALLY FIT.
BRING ON THE WINTER, FATHER...
IN IT'S TIME
WITH IT'S CHILLING ICE AND SNOW.
FOR IT'S ONLY FOR A SEASON
WHILE OUR BLESSINGS
CONTINUE TO FLOW!

EVER SO GENTLY

EVER SO GENTLY THE DAY SLIPS AWAY.
THINKING ABOUT ALL THE EVENTS OF THE DAY. SOME WERE
SURPRISING, ANTICIPATED, SOME NEGATIVES,
SOME POSITIVES TOO.
"AS THE DAY BEGAN, HEAVENLY FATHER, MY THOUGHTS
WERE ON YOU. YOUR AWESOME CREATIVE POWERS FROM
THE RISING TO THE SETTING OF THE SUN. THE SWEET
MELODIOUS SOUNDS OF THE BIRDS CHIRPING, FLOWERS,
BLOOMING, UNIQUE BEAUTY TO EACH AND EVERY ONE.
I THINK OF HOW YOU LOVED ME AND KNEW BE EVEN BEFORE
MY INFANT BIRTH...HOW YOU SACRIFICED YOUR ONLY SON
FOR ALL OF US, EVEN THOSE WHO HAD NO WORTH.
HOW YOU GAVE US YOUR WORD AS A MANUAL FOR DAILY
LIVING THAT TEACHES US HOW TO LIVE AND LOVE, EVEN TO
BE CHEERFUL IN OUR GIVING.
I THINK OF YOUR MERCIES, NEW EACH MORNING AND YOUR
GRACE EXTENDING THROUGH THE NIGHT. YOUR PROVISIONS,
HEALING, STRENGTH AND COMFORT EVEN WHEN OUR
CHOICES ARE NOT ALWAYS RIGHT.
OH, HOW YOU SO GENTLY LEAD US TOWARDS PEACE AND
AWAY FROM STRIFE. THANKS, PRAISE AND WORSHIP TO YOU
UNCEASINGLY OUR MANTRA SHOULD ALWAYS BE.
AS EVER SO GENTLY THE DAYS
AND YES, THE YEARS OF OUR LIFE
COME AND GO...THEN SLIP AWAY.

LAMENTATIONS 3:20-23

MY SOUL HAST THEM STILL IN REMEMBRANCE,
AND IS HUMBLED IN ME.
THIS I RECALL TO MY MIND, THEREFORE HAVE I HOPE.
IT IS OF THE LORD'S MERCIES
THAT WE ARE NOT CONSUMED,
BECAUSE HIS COMPASSIONS FAIL NOT.
THEY ARE NEW EVERY MORNING:
GREAT IS THY FAITHFULNESS.
THE LORD IS MY PORTION, SAITH MY SOUL;
THEREFORE, WILL I HOPE IN HIM.

GOD'S PLUMBLINE

TONIGHT, IS SLEEP ELUDING ME FOR A SPECIFIC REASON.
I'VE SOMETIMES RECEIVED WRITINGS IN THE NIGHT
SEASONS. INTERCESSORY PRAYERS HAVE ALREADY BEEN
SENT UP BUT I AM STILL DRINKING FROM THIS "SLEEPLESS"
CUP. I AM WATCHING AND LISTENING TO
ONLINE MESSAGES TONIGHT. I AM BEING ENLIGHTENED
AND ENCOURAGED WHILE THROUGH THE WINDOWS
FLOWS...MOONLIGHT. ONE OF THE MESSAGES TOLD OF
STANDARDS THAT WE NEED...
IN ORDER TO BE MEASURED BY GOD'S PLUMBLINE...
A MESSAGE GIVEN TO AMOS
TO HELP THE PEOPLE STOP IDOL WORSHIP AND GREED.
ALSO, TO MAKE FOLKS AWARE OF THEIR CONDITION OF SIN...
TO HELP THEM STRIVE FOR A STANDARD OF
EXCELLENCE ...TO WALK IN ROYALTY
OFTEN MOVING THEM FROM WHERE THEY HAD ONCE BEEN.
GOD IS LOOKING FOR A PEOPLE
WHO A STANDARD...WILL MEET. NOT TO BE INFLUENCED
BY THE SIN OF IDOLATRY IN THE STREET.
HE WARNED THEM NOT TO MINGLE, OR BE UNEQUALLY
YOKED WITH NONBELIEVERS AND OTHER TRIFELING FOLKS.
.TO BE CAREFUL OF COMPROMISE WITH ONE FOOT OUT AND
ONE FOOT IN. TOTAL COMMITMENT
IS THE STANDARD AS WE STRIVE TO AVOID SIN.

GOD WILL TAKE US BACK IF WE SLIP INTO DISOBEDIENCE TO
HIS WORD. IF WE HAVE ACCEPTED JESUS,
HIS SON, AS OUR LORD. GOD IS FAITHFUL
AND PROMISED US STRENGTH TO ENDURE
AS MORNING BY MORNING, HE SENDS MERCIES MORE AND
MORE. FOLLOW THROUGH AND DEPENDABILITY
LOYAL CONSISTENT ACCOUNTABILITY
AS WE TOE THAT PLUMB LINE WALKING RESPECTFULLY.
WE ALL FALL DOWN AT ONE TIME OR ANOTHER.
BUT IF WE REPENT GOD WILL PICK US UP
WETHER SISTER OR BROTHER.
WORSHIP IS RECOGNIZING WHO GOD IS.
WE WORSHIP AS A PARTICIPATER NOT A SPECTATOR.
LORD I WORSHIP AND ADORE YOU,
PLACING NO ONE OR NO THING BEFORE YOU.
THE TIME HAS COME FOR US
TO WORSHIP IN SPIRIT AND IN TRUTH.
RECOGNIZING HIM AS OMNICIENT, SOVERIEGN...
AS HE IS ALTOGETHER LOVELY.
WE CAN ONLY MEASURE UP THROUGH FORGIVENESS,
HONESTY, TRUTH AND LOVE.
AS WE WALK IN ROYALTY, LINING UP TO GOD'S STANDARD,
WITH THE DIVINE PLUMBLINE SPECIFIED IN HIS HOLY WORD...
THAT HAS INSPIRED WRITINGS
THROUGH OTHERS FROM HIS HOME IN HEAVEN ABOVE.

HEART NOT EASILY BROKEN

MY HEART IS NOT AS EASILY BROKEN AS IT WAS BEFORE.
SPIRITUAL COPING SKILLS AND FAITH
MAKE ME STRONGER
AS I AM ABLE NOW...TO ENDURE...
AND ACCEPT THE FACT THAT I
CANNOT FIX EVERYTHING OR EVERYONE
OR EVEN TRY TO CARE ABOUT EVERYTHING OR EVERYONE
IS FINALLY SOAKING IN TO MY SPIRIT EACH DAY...
FULL CASTING OF THEIR CARES ON JESUS
IS A FAR BETTER WAY.
SO, THANK GOD FOR TOUGHENING ME...
FOR SETTING ME STRAIGHT THROUGH YOUR WORD AGAIN
SO THAT MY HEART IS NOT AS EASILY BROKEN
AS FORMERLY IT HAD BEEN.
THANK YOU, FATHER, FOR YOUR WORD
TO CONTINUE TO ACKNOWLEDGE YOU
AS TRUST IS STILL MY MANTRA...
AND YES...IT IS HELPING ME THROUGH!

LET THE WAVES ROLL

"JUST TAKE A DEEP BREATH AND LET THE WAVES ROLL"
WASHING AWAY ALL NEGATIVITY
THAT WOULD LODGE IN YOUR SOUL.
THE CLEAR UNADULTERATED BEAUTY
IS SO EASILY SEEN WITH THE NAKED EYE.
TAKE A MOMENT TO LOOK INWARD
AS YOU VIEW COLORS OF THE SKY.
ORANGE, RED, PURPLE, GREEN AND GREY.
SPANNING THE HORIZON COMPLETELY...
ABOVE THE ROLLING WAVES...JUST AS IN LIFE'S SEA.
THE TIDE BRINGS IN SAND, STONE, AND DEPOSITS DEBRIDE,
THEN TAKES OUT WITH IT
SHELLS AND SAND PARTICLES THAT THE EYE CANNOT SEE.
LIFE BRINGS TO US POSITIVES AND NEGATIVES TOO.
WHICH EVER ONE "GROWS" US
IS DEPENDENT ON ME AND YOU.
IT'S ALL A GLORIOUS PART OF GOD'S PERFECT PLAN
ROLLING WAVES AND SIFTING THE EARTH
HE CREATED FOR CREATURES AND FOR MAN.

MUSINGS RE THE EYE

PARAPHRASED...SCRIPTURE TELLS US... THE EYE
IS A LAMP OF THE BODY RADIATING LIGHT TO THE SOUL...
OR IT CAN EMIT A DARKNESS WITHIN
THAT IS DIFFICULT TO KEEP UNDER OUR CONTROL.
THE EYE REVEALS OUR "REAL SELF"
WHETHER OUR HEART HAS WARMTH OR IS COLD.
WHAT OUR EYE SEES
MAKES AN INSTANT IMPRINT ON OUR BRAIN.
WHICH WHEN RECALLED... ENHANCES POSITIVITY
OR REVEALS WHAT WE DISDAIN.
THEREFORE, WE SHOULD SERIOUSLY REGULATE
WHAT WE ALLOW OUR EYES TO VIEW.
FOR THERE WILL BE A NEGATIVE OR POSITIVE EFFECT
ON US OR OTHERS AS WE ARE STRIVING TO GO THROUGH.
IF A MAN CANNOT LOOK TO YOU
EYE TO EYE AS HE SPEAKS
HE SHOULD HAVE LITTLE OR NO IMPACT
ON YOUR PSYCHE, NO MATTER WHAT HE MIGHT SEEK.
THE EYE IS A UNIQUE IDENTIFYING FACTOR.
FOR WHICH DUPLICATION CANNOT BE ACHIEVED.
IT CAN ABSORB LIGHT, REFLECT LIGHT
OR DISPERSE LIGHT TO OTHERS AS WE SPEAK TO THEM,
AT TIMES REVEALING IF WE ARE INDEED A FRIEND.
THE SONG SAYS, "TURN YOUR EYES UPON JESUS
LOOK FULL IN HIS WONDERFUL FACE...AND THE
THINGS OF THIS EARTH WILL GROW SLIGHTLY DIM
IN THE LIGHT OF HIS GLORY AND GRACE".

LAUGHTER IS GOOD LIKE A MEDICINE!!
BODY GOING SOUTH.?

I AM REMINDED IN YOUR WORD, LORD THAT
WHEN EVERYTHING IN THE BODY BEGINS TO GO SOUTH
AND FEW ORIGINAL TEETH REMAIN IN OUR MOUTH...
WE ARE STILL WONDERFULLY
AND FEARFULLY MADE BY YOU...
STILL UNIQUE, HIGHLY FAVORED
BEING LED AS WE GO THROUGH.
WE SMILE AND TELL OTHERS
WE ARE BLESSED AND HIGHLY FAVORED
AS WE STRIVE TO WALK IN FAITH
EXHIBITING GODLY BEHAVIOR.
HIGHLY FAVORED WAS MARY, THE MOTHER OF OUR LORD.
WITH THAT FAVOR CAME MANY EARTHLY HEARTACHES
AND PAIN OF SEPARATION
BEFORE BEING IN POSITION FOR HER HEAVENLY REWARD.
WHEN THE ANGEL TOLD HER THE CHILD SHOULD BE CALLED
JESUS...EMMANUEL, GOD WITH US...
SHE HAD NO IDEA HOW MUCH
HER LIFE WOULD BE ENHANCED BY HER TRUST.
THE WORD TELLS US TO TRUST IN THE LORD
WITH ALL YOUR HEART,
LEANING NOT TO YOUR OWN UNDERSTANDING.
IN ALL YOUR WAYS ACKNOWLEDGE GOD ALLOWING HIM
TO DIRECT AND DO THE PLANNING.
SO, WE MUST NOT EVALUATE
OUR VALUE BY WHAT OUR BODY SHOWS.
WE MUST HOLD OUR HEAD UP...
ENCOURAGE OTHERS AND BE "REAL" ...
GIVING THANKS IN ALL THINGS
NO MATTER HOW WE MIGHT PHYSICALLY FEEL.
NO MATTER WHAT DIRECTION OUR BODY IS ADJUSTING TO
OR WHAT NEGATIVE CHANGES OUR TEETH, STOMACH,
LUNGS, ETC. ARE GOING THROUGH. WHEN WE GIVE THANKS
TO OUR GOD IN ALL THINGS, HE FULFILLS HIS WORD TO US
AND MULTITUDES OF BLESSINGS
IT WILL SURELY BRING.

SHARING ADVERSITY

SHARING ADVERSITY DREW ME
CLOSER TO GOD AND TO DAVID, MY BROTHER...
COMPLETELY CASTING ALL ON HIM
FOR SURELY THERE WAS HOPE IN NONE OTHER.
JUST WITNESSING HIS FAITH IN GOD
WHILE INTERNALIZING HIS COMPLETE DEPENDENCE ON ME
STRENGTHENED MY EFFORTS TO ENHANCE HIS LIFE
UNTIL GOD SET HIM COMPLETELY FREE.
AT TIMES IT SEEMED THAT MY ADVOCATE POSITION
LEFT ME FEELING UNSETTLED AND ALONE.
AS THE BUCK FROM CAREGIVERS WAS PASSED TO AND FRO
LIKE A DOG CHASING AFTER A BONE.
I STAUNCHLY FOUGHT SO MANY BATTLES
THAT WERE CLEARLY OUT OF MY CONTROL.
BEFORE REALIZING THAT THEY WERE TAKING THEIR TOLL.
THERE WERE THOSE WHO WALKED THE JOURNEY WITH US.
WHO MADE EVERY EFFORT TO UNDERSTAND.

WHO ENHANCED HIS LIFE WITH THEIR PRAYERS AND SERVICE
AS THEY OBSERVED ME WALKING WITH HIM...
HOLDING HIS HAND.
HIS CLOSEST BOND WAS TO OUR SISTER AND OUR MOTHER
WHO LEFT US MANY YEARS AGO.
EVEN THROUGH THOSE PRIOR YEARS
HIS DEPENDENCE ON ME WAS DESTINED TO GROW.
GOD BLESSED WITH SIBLINGS, FRIENDS AND NEIGHBORS
WITHOUT WHOSE SUPPORT
IT WOULD HAVE BEEN IMPOSSIBLE
TO WALK COMFORTABLY WITH HIM THROUGH HIS LAST MILE.
TO ENJOY READING AND SINGING WITH HIM
AND HIS LOVE FOR PLAYING GUITAR,
LOVE OF PEOPLE, AND NATURE,
ALSO, THAT OFT TIMES MISCHEVIOUS SMILE.
EVEN SO, SHARING ADVERSITY
DREW ME CLOSER TO GOD AND TO MY BROTHER
REINFORCED COMPLETE RELIANCE ON GOD...
FOR THERE WAS NO HOPE IN ANY OTHER.

TEMPTATIONS/TRIALS

GOD DOES NOT SEND TEMPTATIONS.
TEMPTATIONS ARE SATAN'S PLOYS.
HE TEMPTS US WITH WHAT HE KNOWS
ARE OUR HIDDEN DESIRES...
HIS AIM
IS "OUR WITNESS" TO DESTROY.
GOD SENDS US TRIALS.
AS THE PREACHER RECENTLY SAID,
TRIALS HAVE A PURPOSE
FOR THOSE WHO ARE SPIRIT LED.
THE AIM OF TRIALS ARE
IN SOME CASES, FOR "CORRECTION."
ON THE OTHER HAND, THE AIM
CAN CERTAINLY BE FOR OUR "PERFECTION."
SEEK GOD FOR THE SPECIFIC PURPOSE
OF TRIALS THAT CURRENTLY AFFECT YOU.
THE QUESTION TODAY...
"IS GOD PRESENTLY CORRECTING OR PERFECTING"
OUR WALK AS WE ARE "GOING THROUGH"?

*****

**NOT TO THE SWIFT
IS THE BATTLE.
NOT TO THE STRONG
IS THE RACE.
BUT TO
THE TRUE AND THE FAITHFUL
VICTORY IS PROMISED
THROUGH GRACE
THE JOY OF THE LORD
IS YOUR STRENGTH!**

A WORD FOR TODAY
GRACE, MERCY AND PEACE
(EXCERPTS FROM OUR DAILY BREAD)

GRACE IS WHAT OUR HOLY GOD GIVES US
THAT WE AS SINFUL PEOPLE DO NOT DESERVE.
HE GIVES TO ALL… LIFE BREATH AND
DARKEST HOUR STRENGTH WITHOUT RESERVE.
MERCY IS WHEN GOD WITH HOLDS THAT
WHICH WE DO DESERVE…
THROUGH THE LORD'S MERCIES
"WE ARE NOT CONSUMED"
SO SAYS HIS HOLY WORD.
EVEN AS WAYWARD CHILDREN GOD GIVES TIME
AND HELP FOR US TO TURN BACK TO HIM.
HE PATIENTLY WAITS AS A KIND HEAVENLY FATHER,
PROTECTOR, SHEPHERD, GUIDE AND FRIEND.
PEACE IS WHAT GOD BRINGS TO HIS PEOPLE.
JESUS SAID "PEACE I LEAVE WITH YOU,
MY PEACE I GIVE TO YOU,
NOT AS THE WORLD GIVES DO I GIVE TO YOU."
EVEN IN THE WORST OF TIMES
WE HAVE GOD CONTROLLED
TRANQUILITY AS HE GENTLY WALKS US THROUGH.
BECAUSE GOD REMAINS IN CONTROL
WE CAN BE ENCOURAGED, MY FAMILY, MY FRIENDS.
FOR THROUGHOUT OUR LIVES, IF WE ASK,
HE WILL GIVE US
THE GRACE…
THE MERCY…
THE PEACE…
THAT WE ALL NEED TO CONTINUE TO LIVE FOR HIM.
GOD'S GRACE IS IMMEASURABLE!
HIS MERCY IS INEXHAUSTABLE!
HIS COMFORT AND PEACE IS INEXPRESSABLE!

THE BAND WAGON

NO LONGER DO I WANT TO RIDE THE BAND WAGON.
I PREFER TO WALK ALONG ... BY IT'S SIDE
IMPARTING WISDOM AND ENCOURAGEMENT
AS THE HOLY SPIRIT LEADS AND GUIDES
THE SPOTLIGHT HAS NEVER BEEN MY M.O.
ALTHOUGH FOR SUCCESS I'VE ALWAYS STRIVED.
FROM PUSHING OTHERS TO DO THEIR BEST
MORE PLEASURE I DERIVE.
THE LONGEST MEASURE OF THIS LIFE
I HAVE ALREADY WALKED.
BUT STILL LOOKING FORWARD TO ENJOY
THOSE THINGS OF WHICH I'VE TALKED.
SO THOSE OF YOU STILL RIDING
THE BAND WAGON OF THIS LIFE ON EARTH
AIM HIGH, ACHIEVE YOUR GOALS,
WITH GUSTO AND SELF WORTH.
MAKE GOD THE LEADER
NOT JUST A PARTNER IN YOUR PLANS
DELVE DEEPLY IN HIS WORD
THE HOLY SPIRIT WILL HELP YOU UNDERSTAND.
I HAVE JUMPED OFF THE BAND WAGON
CONTENT IN WALKING BY IT'S SIDE.
GOD HELP ME TO IMPART
WISDOM AND LESSONS LEARNED
FROM ALLOWING
THE HOLY SPIRIT TO LEAD AND GUIDE.

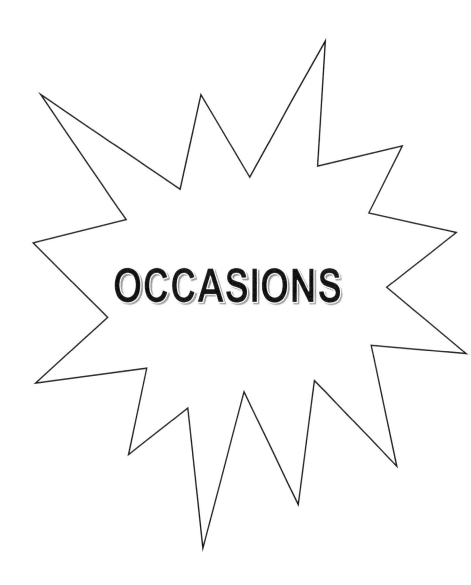

OCCASIONS

THE ETERNAL ROCK (BIRTHDAY AFFIRMATION)
ISAIAH 26:4

I TRUST IN THE LORD GOD ALWAYS. FOR
THE LORD GOD IS THE ETERNAL ROCK.
I WANT TO DISPLAY AN ATTITUDE OF POSITIVITY.
IN OBEDIENCE LET ME WALK MY TALK.
I RECOMMIT MYSELF TO HIM, LEAN ON HIM...
IN HIM...HOPE CONFIDENTLY.
I WILL NOT BE ENTANGLED WITH TROUBLES OF THIS WORLD.
I WILL TRUST IN GOD...MY ROCK...
THE ONE WHO HAS SET ME FREE.
AS MY ROCK HE GAVE ME THE OPPORTUNITY
TO ACCEPT JESUS, PERSONALLY,
AS REDEEMER...AS MY FRIEND.
I HAVE THAT ROCK TO GUIDE ME THROUGH MY END.
MY ROCK GIVES ME
INNER PEACE THAT PASSES ALL UNDERSTANDING.
I CAN CONTINUE TO CLAIM GOD
AS MY FATHER, JESUS AS MY SAVIOR,
THE HOLY SPIRIT TO GUIDE ME
AND HELP ME CHANGE MY BEHAVIOR.
HE IS OUR ETERNAL ROCK. OUR ROCK
DOES NOT ALWAYS MAKE THE ROAD EASY FOR US.
BUT WE CAN BE VICTORIOUS
THROUGH HIM IN WHOM WE'VE PLACED OUR TRUST.
OUR ROCK SENT HIS SON TO DIE FOR US
SO THAT WE COULD HAVE AN ADVOCATE...
AN INTERCESSOR SITTING
AT THE RIGHT OF OUR FATHER'S THRONE.
TO ASK GOD TO GRANT MERCY
INSTEAD OF GIVING US WHAT WE DESERVE...
TO DIRECT GOD'S ATTENTION TO OUR REQUESTS...TO
FULFILL HIS PROMISE
THAT WE'LL NEVER AGAIN BE ALONE.
THANK YOU, FATHER...OUR ETERNAL ROCK
WHO HAS GIVEN US
THE BLESSED ASSURANCE...
THAT THROUGH LIFE'S FAITH WALK WITH YOU WE'LL HAVE
STRENGTH IN WEAKNESS AND DIVINE ENDURANCE.

BIRTHDAY THANKS

HEAVENLY FATHER,
PRAISE YOUR HOLY AND RIGHTEOUS NAME.
WE HAVE ENTERED A BRAND-NEW YEAR OF LIFE
IN WHICH NOTHING EVER REMAINS THE SAME.
A YEAR WITH A STREAM OF
NEW MERCIES EVERY DAY
WITH A DETERMINATION AND MANTRA OF "TRUST"
TO STEADY AND BRIGHTEN
OUR PRESENT PATHWAY.
SO MANY CHANGES IN OUR
LIVES HAVE TAKEN PLACE.
MAY WE GLEAN FROM YOUR WORD
POSITIVITY, WISDOM, STRENGTH
AND SURE GUIDANCE FOR THIS RACE...
RECOGNIZING OUR DESTINY
IS ALREADY IN YOUR CAPABLE HANDS
MAY WE SUBMIT COMPLETELY TO
THE MANIFESTATION OF YOUR SOVEREIGN PLAN.
BOLDLY, YET HUMBLY MAY WE APPROACH
YOUR THRONE OF GRACE.
PRAISING FREELY AND SINCERELY,
CONTENT IN WHERE WE
HAVE BEEN DIVINELY PLACED.
SO, THANK YOU, AGAIN, HEAVENLY FATHER.
FOR ENTERING US INTO A BRAND-NEW YEAR.
WITH POWER, LOVE, A SOUND MIND
AND AN ABSENCE OF GUILT OR FEAR

BIRTHDAY PRAYER OF DESIRE

FATHER, I DESIRE TO BE WHERE YOU WANT ME TO BE.
I DESIRE TO SAY WHAT YOU WANT ME TO SAY.
I DESIRE TO DO WHAT YOU WANT ME TO DO.
RECOGNIZING FATHER, MY TIME CLOCK IS TICKING.
I ACKNOWLEDGE THAT MY TIMEKEEPER IS YOU!
I HAVE NO DESIRE TO PLAN MY FUTURE
TRYING TO LOOK WAY DOWN THROUGH THE YEARS.
INTERPRETING ALL THE DEEP THINGS OF LIFE
OR VIEWING THE OBVIOUS WITH FEAR.
IS THERE A GIVEN? IS THERE AN OBVIOUS?
DOES THIS PLUS THIS EQUAL THAT?
YOUR WORD SAYS TRUST AND ACKNOWLEDGE
LEANING NOT TO MY OWN UNDERSTANDING.
THAT IS A BIBLICAL FACT.
THAT IF I ADHERE TO THAT ADMONITION
MY PATH WILL BE DIRECTED BY YOU.
SO, I WILL FOLLOW YOUR LEAD ANOTHER YEAR,
THROUGH YOUR SPIRIT.
AND IN CONFIDENCE
I WILL DANCE MY WAY THROUGH!

PHILIPPIANS 4:6
DON'T WORRY ABOUT ANYTHING.
INSTEAD,
PRAY ABOUT EVERYTHING.
TELL GOD WHAT YOU NEED,
AND THANK HIM
FOR ALL HE HAS DONE.

PHILIPPIANS 4:6
DON'T WORRY ABOUT ANYTHING.
INSTEAD,
PRAY ABOUT EVERYTHING.
TELL GOD WHAT YOU NEED,
AND THANK HIM
FOR ALL HE HAS DONE.

BIRTHDAY THANK YOU

MOST GRACIOUS, HOLY, MERCIFUL HEAVENLY FATHER,
GIVER OF LIFE, SALVATION, STABILITY OF MIND,
WITH A BOWED DOWN HEAD, AND A HUMBLE SPIRIT
I POUR OUT MY HEART. ENHANCE FAITH THAT BINDS...
ME CLOSER EVEN CLOSER AS I APPROACH YOU
AS SOVEREIGN ON YOUR THRONE OF GRACE.
THROUGH YOUR HOLY SPIRIT...
DIRECT MY THOUGHTS, ATTITUDES AND GOALS,
THAT I NOT ONLY TAKE UP SPACE.
I DESIRE TO FIT SECURELY AS AN INTEGRAL PIECE
IN YOUR PREDESTINED PUZZLE OF LIFE.
HELP ME TO LIVE YOUR WORD EXPERIENTIALLY AS
A MOTHER, GRAND, SISTER, AUNT, FRIEND, MOST
IMPORTANTLY WIFE AS I DELVE WITH THE HOLY SPIRIT INTO
YOUR BIBLE, SACRED MANUAL FOR LIVING...
BE PRESENT FATHER, SHOW ME, SPEAK TO ME, INSTILL IN ME,
EMBOLDEN AND REASSURE. THANK YOU FOR FORGIVING
ALL OF MY SINS AND IDIOSYNCRASIES
THAT ARE UNPLEASING IN YOUR SIGHT.
I DESIRE TO SHARE LOVE, PATIENCE, KINDNESS,
INTEGRITY AND SPIRITUAL MOTIVATION DAY AND NIGHT.
THANK YOU FOR MY APPROACH TO
ANOTHER MOTHER'S DAY
AND ANOTHER YEAR ON THIS EARTH.
ESTABLISH MY STEPS AND STOPS
AS YOU SECURE AND INCREASE MY WORTH.
THANK YOU FOR MY FAMILY AND
BLOOD WASHED SISTERS AND BROTHERS
WHO COVER ME IN PRAYERS FOR DAILY PROTECTION,
STRENGTH AND INSIGHT INTO SPIRITUAL NEEDS OF OTHERS.
NEVER ALLOW ME FATHER, TO BECOME AS A
SENSELESS, USELESS, INSENSITIVE STUMBLING BLOCK
WITH LIFE'S ACTIONS TURNING ANYONE AWAY INSTEAD
OF TOWARDS YOU AS
THEIR REDEEMER, FORTRESS... THEIR ROCK.
I PRAY THAT YOU WILL TURN HEARTS TOWARDS YOU
THAT ARE STILL STRADDLING THE SPIRITUAL FENCE.
LET THEM BE AWARE OF YOUR HOLY SPIRIT IN THEM
WHOSE EMPOWERMENT HAS NO LENGTH. AMEN

A PRAYER FOR YOUR BIRTHDAY
THANK "THE GREATER"

FATHER, I THANK YOU FOR THE GIFT OF LIFE.
THE GIFT OF DAILY BLESSINGS BEYOND ALL EXPECTATIONS.
THE GIFT OF YOUR PRESENCE,
ASSURANCE OF NEVER BEING ALONE.
THE GIFT OF ETERNAL LIFE
SOMEWHERE AROUND YOUR THRONE.
THE GIFT OF LOVE AND CARE
WITHOUT QUALIFICATIONS NEEDED.
JUST A HUMBLE WILLING SOUL
WHO GOD ANSWERS WHEN ENTREATED.
THE GIFT OF YOUR OMNICIENCE,
KNOWLEDGE OF OUR THINKING.
OMNIPOTENCE WITH ALL POWER TO HOLD US UP
WHEN WE ARE SINKING…
IN SORROW, SICKNESS, DESPAIR, DEPRESSION
THREATENING TO OVERTAKE
AN ATTEMPT TO CONQUER OUR SOUL.
A TECHNIQUE USED BY SATAN TO ATTACK
THOSE WHOSE NAME IS ON GOD'S ROLL.
BUT "GREATER" IS HE WITHIN US
THAN HE WHO DESIRES TO RULE OVER OUR LIFE…
"GREATER" IS HE THAT IS WITHIN US WHO REMOVES
ALL FEAR AND ATTEMPTED STRIFE.
SO, WE NOW
THANK "THE GREATER" AGAIN FOR THE GIFT OF LIFE,
THE GIFT OF SALVATION,
THE GIFT OF DAILY, MERCY,
GRACE AND
ENORMOUS BLESSINGS,
EVEN BEYOND OUR
HIGHEST EXPECTATIONS!

BIRTHDAY HUMOR   HEY...HEY...HEY

TO OUR FATHER WHO DOES ALL THINGS WELL,
LET'S SEND UP SOME PRAISE.
THESE ONE YEAR OLDER, ACHING ARMS,
TO OUR SAVIOR, LET'S JUST RAISE.
PRAISE HIM FOR HIS GOODNESS,
HIS LOVE...HIS GRACE.
PRAISE HIM FOR OUR HISTORY OF
HIS STRENGTH HE'S GIVEN FOR LIFE'S RACE.
DO WE FACE EACH DAY WITH ONLY SUNSHINE
AND NO RAIN IN OUR VIEW?
NOT SO... RAINY DAYS ARE A FACT OF LIFE
BUT GOD WALKS US THROUGH THEM TOO...
WITH THE LOVE AND PROTECTION OF
HIS SON WHO GAVE HIS LIFE FOR US.
LET'S JUST RAISE THESE TIRED OLD ARMS
AS A SYMBOL OF OUR TRUST...
TO OUR GOD WHO PROMISED TO
NEVER LEAVE OUR SIDE OR FORSAKE. PRAISE HIM...
PRAISE HIM...PRAISE HIM
EVEN THOUGH ALL OF LIFE IS NOT "A PIECE OF CAKE."
IT'S SOMETIMES FAT AND GRISSLE AND BONE
BUT WE'VE LEARNED TO ENJOY THAT TOO.
PASSED DOWN FROM GENERATIONS
WHOM WE'VE WITNESSED GOD BRINGING THEM THROUGH.
SO, HEY...HEY...HEY
LET'S GIVE GOD SOME PRAISE.
LET'S SING AND SHOUT OUR THANKS
AS THESE TIRED, ONE YEAR OLDER OLD ARMS WE RAISE!!
PROVERBS 17:22. "A MERRY HEART DOETH
GOOD LIKE A MEDICINE

BIRTHDAY GOLDEN YEARS

HAVE YOU BEEN TESTED ...
BY THE FIRE OF GROSS CIRCUMSTANCE?
HAVE YOU FELT AS IF YOU HAVE BEEN MELTED, RESHAPED,
MOLDED, THEN GIVEN ANOTHER CHANCE?
DO YOU FEEL REFORMED, RESTORED,
POLISHED TO A MORE BRILLIANT SHINE?
HAS YOUR FAITH BEEN
ENHANCED WITH TRUST THAT ALL WILL BE FINE?
ARE YOU MORE VALUABLE IN GOD'S KINGDOM...
HUMBLED YET BOLDER?
ARE THE YEARS SEEMINGLY PASSING
MORE QUICKLY AS YOU ARE GROWING OLDER?
WELL THEN, WELCOME TO THE GOLDEN YEARS!

WE HAVE LEARNED...

NO MATTER WHAT THE CIRCUMSTANCE
WE CAN FIND PEACE IN GOD'S PRESENCE.

SOME DAYS JOY IS GENEROUSLY STREWN ALONG LIFE'S
PATH LIKE FLASHES IN THE SUNLIGHT.
THOSE DAYS... CONTENTMENT IS EASY. OUR THOUGHTS ARE
HAPPY OUR BURDENS EVEN SEEM LIGHT.

OTHER DAYS ARE OVERCAST AND GLOOMY. WE FEEL THE
STRESSES OF A JOURNEY THAT SEEMS ENDLESS. WE MIGHT
FEEL ABANDONED AND SOMETIMES EVEN FRIENDLESS.

JOY IS NOT GONE! WE HAVE LEARNED
TO SEARCH FOR IT AS HIDDEN TREASURE...
REMEMBERING GOD CREATED THIS DAY.
NOT A CHANCE OCCURRENCE
FOR HE ALONE IS SOVEREIGN BEYOND MEASURE.

WE RECALL THAT HE IS PRESENT
WHETHER WE SENSE IT OR NOT.

WE HAVE LEARNED

TO START TALKING WITH HIM ABOUT OUR ISSUES,
FEELINGS AND DEEPEST THOUGHTS.
WE EXPERIENCE JOY IN THE FACT
THAT HE UNDERSTANDS US PERFECTLY...
AS WE COMMUNICATE WITH
HIM OUR MOOD LIGHTENS.
AWARENESS OF HIS PRESENCE MAKES US FREE!
FREE FROM WORRIES CONCERNING
THINGS WE DO NOT UNDERSTAND.
FREE... REALIZING WE MUST BE PREPARED
TO LET GO OF ANYTHING HE TAKES FROM US...
ALWAYS GIVING PRAISE BECAUSE...
WITHOUT A DOUBT HE CONTINUES TO HOLD OUR HAND.
WE HAVE LEARNED

TO COME BOLDLY TO HIS THRONE
TO OBTAIN GRACE AND MERCY.
THAT ABIDING IN HIM AND INTERNALIIZING HIS WORD IN US
WILL LIGHTEN OUR JOURNEY, MULTIPLY OUR
FAITH...INCREASE OUR TRUST.
WE HAVE LEARNED

TO YIELD TO HIM OUR BODY AND SOUL
RECOGNIZING THAT HE ALONE IS IN TOTAL CONTROL.
WE HAVE BEEN... AS GOLD... MELTED, TESTED,
MOLDED, RESHAPED, RESTORED.
SO YES, THESE ARE OUR GOLDEN YEARS....
GOLDEN YEARS...BRING THEM ON...
FOR WITH GOD
WE CAN AND WE WILL...
PROCEED... WITHOUT FEAR!

ISAIAH 46:4 NIV

**EVEN TO YOUR OLD AGE AND GRAY HAIRS I AM HE, I AM HE
WHO WILL SUSTAIN YOU. I HAVE MADE YOU AND I WILL
CARRY YOU; I WILL SUSTAIN YOU AND I WILL RESCUE YOU.**

NEW YEAR PRAYER

I THANK GOD FOR THIS WINTERTIME.
ANOTHER YEAR HAS PASSED.
NEW TOMORROWS, NEW CHALLENGES, FATHER,
PREPARE ME FOR NEW TASKS.
YOUR WORD SAYS, "SEARCH MY HEART OH GOD,
TEST MY THOUGHTS,
POINT OUT TO ME IF I OFFEND THEE.
LEAD ME THROUGH THE PATH
OF LIFE EVERLASTING "
WITH PRAISE, WORSHIP AND THANKS
OFFERED FREELY.
EMPOWER ME WITH WISDOM
TO LIVE EACH DAY PLEASING TO YOU.
DIRECT MY STEPS, MY STOPS, CONVERSATIONS,
ACTIONS AND REACTIONS TOO.
CONTINUE TO SEND PROTECTIVE ANGELS
TO SURROUND ME EVERY DAY.
HELP ME TO RECOGNIZE YOUR SPIRIT'S PROMPTINGS
AS I TRAVEL ON LIFE'S WAY.
THANK YOU, HEAVENLY FATHER
AGAIN, I OFFER THANKS TO YOU.
SHOW ME NUGGETS IN YOUR HOLY WORD
THAT WILL HELP ME TO GO THROUGH.

CELEBRATE WITH JOY

JESUS NO LONGER
LIES IN THE MANGER ON THE HAY.
HE NOW
DWELLS ON HIGH
MAKING INTERCESSION EACH DAY
FOR ALL
WHO WILL ACCEPT HIS PLAN
OF SALVATION AND LOVE
HE SENDS PERPETUAL GUIDANCE FROM ABOVE.
HE SENDS INNER PEACE
THROUGH HIS HOLY SPIRIT DIVINE
THAT'S BEYOND UNDERSTANDING
IN OUR FINITE MIND.
AS WE CELEBRATE WITH JOY
THIS GLORIOUS SEASON
MAY THE BIRTH OF CHRIST IN YOUR HEART
BE
THE MOST
IMPORTANT
REASON.

CHRISTMAS SEASON

CHRISTMAS SEASON IS DRAWING NEAR
A GLORIOUS CELEBRATION BUT TO SOME IT IS DREAR.
THEY WONDER IF DECEMBER TWENTY-FIFTH WAS THE DAY
OF OUR SAVIOR'S BIRTH OR WAS IT NOVEMBER OR JANUARY
WHEN HE WAS SENT TO EARTH?
OTHER QUESTIONS HAPPEN TO BE...
IF HIS HAIR WAS WOOL TEXTURED
IF HIS COUNTENANCE WAS SWEET.
HISTORIANS, BIBLE SCHOLARS, PRIEST,
HAVE ALL STUDIED THIS EVENT.
VARIOUS CONCLUSIONS HAVE BEEN REACHED.
HIS SKIN COLOR WAS "OLIVE" SO THE "GOOD BOOK" STATES.
HE WAS NOT FAIR OR BLUE EYED
WITH BLONDE HAIR THAT WAS STRAIGHT.
JUST NOTICE THE PEOPLE THAT CAME FROM HIS HOMELAND.
THEN LOOK IN "GOD'S WORD"
FOR THE TRUE NATURE OF "THE MAN."
JUST HOW MUCH TIME AND EMPHASIS
OR ASSUMPTION SHOULD WE PLACE...
HOW IMPORTANT...CALENDAR OR COLOR...
SPECIFIC TIME OR PLACE?
WE OFTEN GET CAUGHT UP IN TECHNICALITIES,
WE'RE LOSING THE ESSENCE OF CHRIST IN TECHNICALITIES,
I FEAR., WE'RE LOSING THAT TRUE ESSENCE AS THIS
HOLIDAY DRAWS NEAR.

...

JESUS, OUR SAVIOR, BY GOD WAS SENT TO EARTH.
HE WAS BORN IN A MANGER. A MOST HUMBLE BIRTH.
FOR MORE THAN TWO DECADES HE WAS TAUGHT BY
PARENTS AND TEMPLE PRIESTS.
OBEDIENCE TO THEM AND "HIS FATHER"
THROUGHOUT HIS LIFE NEVER CEASED.
AS HE WALKED AMONG MEN,
TEACHING, HEALING...MIRACLES HE WORKED.
HE PREPARED DISCIPLES AND OTHERS
FOR HIS DEPARTURE FROM OUR EARTH.
HE WAS DESTINED TO DIE ON AN OLD RUGGED CROSS
THEN HE AROSE FROM THE TOMB
SO, OUR LIVES WOULD NOT BE LOST...
TO ADDICTIONS, EVIL THOUGHTS, OR A STRUGGLE
FOR POWER.WE NEED ONLY TO ACCEPT HIM...
ETERNAL LIFE WILL BE OURS.
THIS MESSAGE IS CONTROVERSIAL
BUT BACKED UP BY "HIS WORD."
SEARCH THE SCRIPTURES FOR YOURSELF.
GET TO KNOW JESUS AS LORD.
ACCEPT HIS PROTECTION, AND GUIDANCE
AND HE'LL BE YOUR DEAREST FRIEND.
FAITH AND PEACE OF MIND WILL FOLLOW
FOR HIS LOVE KNOWS NO END.
SO, HOWEVER YOU VIEW THESE STATEMENTS OR YOUR
MODE OF WORSHIP OR BELIEF.
REMEMBER TO PLACE CHRIST FIRST IN YOUR LIFE AND HIS
BLESSINGS YOU'LL RECEIVE.
AND I PRAY THAT AS WE PAY TRIBUTE TO HIM
SHARING GIFTS OF HEARTFELT LOVE
WE'LL ALSO TAKE TIME TO GIVE HONOR AND PRAISE TO OUR
WONDERFUL FATHER ABOVE.

REGARDING HOLLY BUSHES

WE CELEBRATE THE BIRTH OF JESUS
WHO IS NO LONGER IN THE MANGER ON THE HAY
 BUT SITS ON THE RIGHT SIDE OF HIS FATHER GOD, MAKING
INTERCESSION EACH DAY... FOR THOSE
FOR WHOM HE WORE THAT CROWN OF THORNS.
WHEN WE VIEW HOLLY AT THIS HOLY TIME OF YEAR
 MAY WE REMEMBER ITS SHARP LEAVES WERE SAID TO
SYMBOLIZE CHRIST'S CROWN OF THORNS
AND ITS RED BERRIES
THE BLOOD HE SHED FOR THE REMISSION OF SIN.
THE HOLLY BUSH WITH THE SNOWFLAKE STAR ON TOP ALSO
WITH IT'S DEEP GREEN SHINY LEAVES
SPIRITUALLY REPRESENTS JESUS, THE LIGHT OF THIS WORLD...
THE ONLY ONE WHO GRANTS FORGIVENESS, ABUNDANT LIFE,
MERCY, GRACE, PROTECTION, COMFORT, HEALING
AND A MYRIAD OF BLESSINGS RECORDED IN HIS HOLY WORD
TO ALL WHO WILLINGLY RECEIVE HIM
AS PERSONAL SAVIOR & LORD.

A GET-WELL...DECLARATION OF TRUST
FATHER, I TRUST YOU

HEAVENLY FATHER, I TRUST YOU.
THAT IS ALL I CAN SAY. FATHER, I TRUST YOU.
YOU ARE THE ONLY WAY.
YOUR WORD SAYS TRUST,
LEANING NOT TO MY OWN UNDERSTANDING.
I ALSO ACKNOWLEDGE YOU IN ALL MY WAYS
LOOKING UP TO YOU FOR DIVINE PLANNING.
REMOVING OBSTACLES IN LIFE IS WHAT YOU DO...
WHILE STRENGTHENING, HEALING, GUIDING
ALL OF YOUR CHILDREN THROUGH.
GRANTING GRACE, PEACE
AND MERCY...DAY BY DAY.
ENLIGHTENING US THROUGH YOUR WORD
AND HEARING US WHEN WE PRAY.
ABIDING IN YOU AND ALLOWING
YOUR WORD TO ABIDE IN US.
ENABLES US TO GIVE YOU OUR BURDENS
WHILE ENHANCING OUR TRUST.
YOUR WORD SAYS WHEN WE'VE
DONE ALL TO STAND...STAND.
WITH CONFIDENCE...BECAUSE YOU WILL CONTINUE
TO HOLD TIGHTLY TO OUR HAND.
SO, FATHER, I CONTINUE TO
TO TRUST YOU...
THERE IS NO OTHER WAY.
FATHER I CONTINUE TO TRUST YOU.
THAT IS ALL I CAN SAY!
AMEN

HOPE GET WELL

ROMANS 15:13 TLB

SO, I PRAY THAT GOD,
WHO GIVES YOU **HOPE** WILL KEEP YOU HAPPY
AND FULL OF PEACE AS YOU BELIEVE IN HIM.
MAY YOU OVERFLOW WITH
HOPE
THROUGH THE POWER OF THE HOLY SPIRIT.

NOW FAITH IS THE SUBSTANCE OF THINGS
HOPED FOR...
THE EVIDENCE OF THINGS NOT SEEN.

- HOPE IN THE LORD WHO CREATED YOU!
- OPERATE IN THE FULLNESS OF HIS SPIRIT
- PRAY WITHOUT CEASING
- ENERGIZE YOURSELF THROUGH READING AND STUDY
- OF HIS WORD.

WHILE YOU ARE CONTINUING TO RECUPERATE
FOCUS ON **HOPE , HEALING,**
THANKFULNESS,
PRAISE AND
THE LOVE OF GOD WHO GIVES US
INNER PEACE AND A FUTURE AS
YOU CONTINUE TO HOPE IN HIM!!

PSALM 149:1&3A TLB

YES, PRAISE THE LORD! SING HIM A NEW SONG.
SING HIS PRAISES ALL YE PEOPLE.
PRAISE HIS NAME WITH DANCING
ACCOMPANIED BY DRUMS AND LYRE.

HALLELUJAH NO CANCER

HALLELUJAH FOR THE SHED BLOOD OF JESUS CHRIST
THAT PROVIDED REDEMPTION FOR
COMMITTED...SAVED...LIVES.
HALLELUJAH FOR THE SHED BLOOD OF JESUS CHRIST
WHOSE HOLY SPIRIT PROVIDES PROTECTION
AND DAILY NEW STRENGTH FOR THE STRIVE.
HALLELUJAH FOR YOUR CONTINUAL FAITH WALK TODAY
FOR THE YEARS YOU HAVE WALKED
WITH GOD IN HIS WAY
HALLELUJAH FOR THE SHED BLOOD OF CHRIST OUR LORD
THAT WASHED CLEAN OUR SOULS
AND PROVIDED CREDENCE TO HIS WORD.
YES, GLORY HALLELUJAH FOR THE SHED BLOOD
OF JESUS CHRIST OUR LORD
IT HUMBLES...REINFORCES FAITH
AS NEW MIRACLES OUR MINDS ABSORB.
THANK YOU...THANK YOU FATHER
FOR THE SACRIFICE OF YOUR ONLY SON
WHICH PROVIDED A WAY OF ESCAPE
FOR EACH AND EVERY ONE.

CACTUS GET WELL THOUGHTS

YOU'RE ENHANCING YOUR SPIRITUAL VALUES
LONG AGO ACCEPTING THE GIFT OF GOD'S SON.
YOU'VE TAKEN THAT RELATIONSHIP SERIOUSLY
AS SOME LIFE BATTLES WERE LOST
BUT MORE HAVE BEEN WON.
AS THE CACTUS IN OUR YARD
SOME PATHS BLOSSOMED
AND SOME PATHS PRICKED
BUT THROUGH IT ALL
ALLOW YOUR ZEAL FOR KNOWLEDGE
OF GOD'S WORD TO
STILL CONSTANTLY BLOOM
AS THE CLOCK OF TIME TICKS.

LIFE IS BEAUTIFUL
BUT SOMETIMES
THERE ARE PAINFUL PRICKS.
".

I THESSALONIANS 5:18 KJV
IN EVERYTHING GIVE THANKS FOR THIS
IS THE WILL OF GOD IN CHRIST JESUS
CONCERNING YOU.

WEDDING PRAYER

THANK YOU, HEAVENLY FATHER
FOR THIS VERY SPECIAL WEDDING DAY
BLESS THESE TWO...THAT YOU HAVE JOINED
TO WALK TOGETHER ALL THE WAY.
MAY THEY APPROACH YOUR THRONE OF GRACE
AT THE START OF EACH NEW MORNING
IN PRAISE, AND PETITIONS FOR PROTECTION
THROUGH EVENTS THAT TAKE PLACE WITHOUT WARNING.
MAY THEY WORSHIP YOU TOGETHER
GLEANING INSTRUCTIONS FROM YOUR HOLY WORD.
LET NO SIN ORIGINATE IN ANGER.
MAY THEY FORGIVE AND SEEK YOUR FORGIVENESS...LORD.
"LET NOT THE SUN" EVER ON THEIR WRATH GO DOWN.
MAY THEY SETTLE ALL OPEN ISSUES
WITH YOUR WISDOM THAT IS ALWAYS SOUND.
MAY THEY CONTINUE TO
RAISE THEIR DAUGHTERS AND THEIR SONS,
TEACHING THEM THAT YOU ARE THE ONE
THAT THEY SHOULD ACCEPT
AS THEIR PERSONAL SAVIOR AND FRIEND.
THAT YOU'RE THE ONLY ONE
WHO CAN BE WITH THEM THROUGHOUT THEIR END.
AS THEY ARE GENTLY GUIDED
BY YOUR MIGHTY HAND FROM ABOVE
MAY THEY ACCEPT YOUR MERCY...YOUR PARDON...
YOUR GRACE...AND YOUR LOVE. AMEN

I CORINTHIAN 13:4-13 (THE LIVING BIBLE)

LOVE IS VERY PATIENT AND KIND, NEVER JEALOUS OR
ENVIOUS NEVER BOASTFUL OR PROUD, NEVER HAUGHTY OR
SELFISH OR RUDE. LOVE DOES NOT DEMAND ITS OWN WAY.
IT IS NOT IRRITABLE OR TOUCHY. IT DOES NOT HOLD
GRUDGES AND WILL HARDLY EVEN NOTICE WHEN OTHERS
DO IT WRONG. IT IS NEVER GLAD ABOUT INJUSTICE BUT
REJOICES WHENEVER TRUTH WINS OUT.
IF YOU LOVE
SOMEONE YOU WILL BE LOYAL
TO HIM NO MATTER WHAT THE COST.
YOU WILL ALWAYS BELIEVE IN HIM,
ALWAYS EXPECT THE BEST OF HIM,
AND ALWAYS STAND YOUR GROUND IN DEFENDING HIM.
ALL THE SPECIAL GIFTS AND POWERS FROM GOD WILL
SOMEDAY COME TO AN END, BUT LOVE GOES ON FOREVER.
SOMEDAY PROPHECY, AND SPEAKING IN UNKNOWN
LANGUAGES, AND SPECIAL KNOWLEDGE...
THESE GIFTS WILL DISAPPEAR.
NOW WE KNOW SO LITTLE, EVEN WITH OUR SPECIAL GIFTS,
AND THE PREACHING OF THOSE MOST GIFTED IS STILL SO
POOR. BUT WHEN WE HAVE BEEN MADE PERFECT AND
COMPLETE, THEN THE NEED FOR THOSE
INADEQUATE SPECIAL GIFTS WILL COME TO AN END,
AND THEY WILL DISAPPEAR. IT'S LIKE THIS:
WHEN I WAS A CHILD, I SPOKE AND THOUGHT AND
REASONED AS A CHILD DOES. BUT WHEN I BECAME A MAN,
MY THOUGHTS GREW FAR BEYOND THOSE OF MY
CHILDHOOD, AND NOW I HAVE PUT AWAY THE CHILDISH
THINGS. IN THE SAME WAY, WE CAN SEE AND
UNDERSTAND ONLY A LITTLE ABOUT GOD NOW, AS IF WE
WERE PEERING AT HIS REFLECTION IN A POOR MIRROR; BUT
SOMEDAY WE ARE GOING TO SEE HIM IN HIS COMPLETENESS,
FACE TO FACE. NOW ALL THAT I KNOW IS HAZY AND
BLURRED, BUT THEN I WILL SEE EVERYTHING CLEARLY,
JUST AS CLEARLY AS GOD SEES INTO MY HEART RIGHT NOW.
THERE ARE THREE THINGS THAT REMAIN...FAITH, HOPE, AND
LOVE...AND THE GREATEST OF THESE IS LOVE.

FEBRUARY LOVE MONTH

OUR PRECIOUS JEWELS

YOU ARE OUR JEWELS. THE ONES THAT WE TREASURE. OUR
LOVE AND PRIDE FOR YOU IS FAR ABOVE MEASURE.
WE PRAY EACH ONE OF YOU WILL KNOW JESUS AS YOUR
LORD. TO HELP YOU HERE ON EARTH
AND GRANT HEAVENLY REWARD.
WE PRAY THAT YOU WILL OBEY GOD
AND YOUR PARENTS ABOVE ALL OTHERS.
THAT YOUR SELF RESPECT
WILL FLOW TO SISTERS AND TO BROTHERS.
FOR IT'S SO IMPORTANT
TO CONTINUE TO HAVE SELF RESPECT.
IT WILL RAISE YOU FAR ABOVE THE CROWD
AND YOU WILL NEVER REGRET…
THE CHOICES, THAT IN LIFE
YOU ARE CALLED TO MAKE.
YOU MIGHT BEND AS YOU WALK THROUGH
BUT IF YOU TRUST GOD
YOU WILL NOT BREAK.
ALWAYS THINK, PRAY, STUDY,
THEN FACE LIFE'S CHALLENGES
HEAD ON…ONE BY ONE.
SHOULDERS AND HEAD UP. LOOK DIRECTLY
INTO EYES, SPEAK HONESTLY
UNTIL EACH TASK IS DONE.

WE WILL ALWAYS LOVE YOU
OUR GRANDS,
OUR PRECIOUS
JEWELS OF LOVE.
FOR YOU, WE THANK
OUR GOD ABOVE.

145

FATHER'S DAY SO GLAD

WE ARE SO GLAD THAT
YOU ARE "SECURE IN HIM" …
THAT LONG AGO YOU ACCEPTED JESUS
TO BE YOUR CLOSEST FRIEND.
THAT HE HAS GUIDED YOU AND KEPT YOU
AS YOU HELPED RAISE YOUR PRECIOUS FAMILY.
THAT YOU HAVE EXCELLED AS A FATHER!
OH, WE GIVE GOD...ALL OF THE PRAISE!

WE'RE GLAD FOR OUR GRANDS
THAT THEY HAVE A FATHER SUCH AS YOU.
WHOSE CONCERN, EXAMPLE,
LOVE AND PRAYERS GO OUT
FOR GOD TO HELP CARRY THEM THROUGH.
WE'RE GLAD YOU WILL REMAIN
INTERESTED AND DELIGHTED IN THEM.
THAT YOU ALWAYS REMAIN "FATHER"
NOT THEIR "BUDDY" BUT STILL THEIR FRIEND.

HOLD ON TO THE PROMISES.
READ THEM DAILY IN HIS WORD.
CONTINUE TO TRUST IN HIM COMPLETELY
TO REMAIN YOUR SAVIOR AND LORD.

CONTINUE TO BE STRONG,
BE STEADFAST...WORSHIP...
BE FAITHFUL, BE TRUE.

ON THIS FATHER'S DAY,
AS ALWAYS
OUR LOVE AND PRIDE

ARE EXTENDED
TO YOU!

ANNIVERSARY

WHAT A HAPPY MORNING,
HEAVENLY FATHER.
ANOTHER ANNIVERSARY IS HERE.
THANK YOU. YOU BLESSED ME
BEFORE I ENTERED THE WOMB.
YOUR PROMISES ARE CLEAR.
YOU HAVE BEEN MY FORTRESS, MY ROCK,
MY HIGH TOWER, MY GUIDE.
UNDER YOUR WINGS OF PROTECTION
I AM PLEASED TO ABIDE.
THANK YOU FOR CHILDHOOD MEMORIES THAT ARE
PLEASANT...THAT I CHERISH.
FOR THE GIFT OF SALVATION
WITH ASSURANCE THAT I'LL NOT PERISH.
THANK YOU FOR INCLUDING
ETERNAL LIFE IN YOUR PROMISES TO ME
AND THE PRESENCE OF YOUR SPIRIT
THAT EMPOWERS MY DESIRE TO BE FREE,
FROM UNFORGIVENESS, ENVY, VAIN PRIDE,
OR THE NEED TO CONTROL.
THANK YOU FOR RELEASING ME
FROM MATTERS
THAT DO NOT THREATEN THE SOUL.

THANK YOU FOR MY LIFE PARTNER.
THAT TOGETHER WE STRIVE
TO LOVE YOU, HONOR YOU,
AND GIVE YOU FIRST PLACE IN OUR LIVES.
THANK YOU FOR AWARENESS
TO ACKNOWLEDGE YOU IN ALL MY WAYS.
FOR SOUND MIND, STRENGTH OF BODY,
AND A HEART THAT'S FILLED WITH PRAISE.
THANK YOU FOR "CHILDREN" AND "GRANDS"
THAT KEEP ME IN THEIR THOUGHTS.
THAT ARE AWARE AND ALSO THANKFUL FOR THE DISTANCE
I'VE BEEN BROUGHT.
THANK YOU FOR FAMILY,
FOR RELATIONSHIPS, FOR FRIENDS
THAT LOVE ME AND ENCOURAGE ME
AS ON YOU...I DEPEND.
FATHER NEVER LET ME BECOME A
STUMBLING BLOCK OR A HYPOCRITE.
KEEP MY MIND "STAYED ON THEE,
THAT I MAY BE SPIRITUALLY FIT.
GRANT MORE WISDOM
THAT IS DISTINCTLY PROMISED IN YOUR WORD,
THAT SAYS WHERE THERE IS LACK...
JUST ASK. MY GOD, MY SAVIOR, MY LORD.
THANK YOU FOR YEARS
OF TOGETHERNESS.
UNTIL I REST WITH YOU IN GLORY...
KEEP MY PATHWAY CLEAR. AMEN

ANNIVERSARY BUTTERFLY

FOR HAPPINESS IS A BUTTERFLY,
WHICH WHEN PURSUED,
IS ALWAYS JUST BEYOND YOUR GRASP,
BUT WHICH,
IF YOU WILL SIT DOWN QUIETLY...
MAY ALIGHT ON YOU. (AUTHOR UNKNOWN)

TOGETHER YOU HAVE SAT DOWN QUIETLY,
EXPERIENCED GLADNESS,
EXPERIENCED SADNESS,
EXPERIENCED UNSPEAKABLE JOY
BASKED IN
THE RISING AND SETTING OF THE SUN
THE OCEAN, SANDY BEACH,
THE RAINBOW OF VARIOUS CIRCUMSTANCES
IN RAISING AND NURTURING
YOUR FAMILY
SO INDEED, THE BUTTERFLY OF HAPPINESS
HAS ALIGHTED ON YOU.
MANY MORE YEARS OF
MARRIAGE BLISS,
HEALTH,
HAPPINESS AND ENLIGHTENMENT AS
YOU CONTINUE TO WALK TOGETHER
IN LOVE AND RESPECT
FOR GOD AND EACH OTHER.

BLESSED AND HIGHLY FAVORED
WOMEN'S DAY OR RETREAT

BLESSED AND HIGHLY FAVORED,
WAS MARY, MOTHER OF THE SON OF GOD.
SHE WAS TOUCHED BY THE HOLY SPIRIT
AS NONE OTHER ON EARTHLY SOD.
WOMEN, TODAY...WE ARE ALSO
BLESSED AND HIGHLY FAVORED.
BY WHOM...FOR WHAT REASON?
BLESSED BY OUR FATHER GOD.
TO BLESS OTHERS IN AND OUT OF SEASON.
WE ARE NOT BLESSED AND HIGHLY FAVORED
BECAUSE WE ARE UNTOUCHED BY MAN...
ONLY CHRIST'S BIRTH, LIFE, DEATH,
RESURRECTION AND ASCENSION
ENABLES US TO STAND.
WE ARE BLESSED AND HIGHLY FAVORED
AS WE ACCEPT JESUS AS OUR LORD...
AS WE YIELD TO HIS HOLY SPIRIT...
AS WE ACCEPT GUIDANCE FROM HIS WORD.
PROVERBS CHAPTER THREE TELL US...
TRUTHFULNESS AND KINDNESS GAINS FAVOR
WITH BOTH GOD AND MAN.
A REPUTATION FOR GOOD JUDGEMENT AND COMMON SENSE.
TRUSTING GOD COMPLETELY
AS WE FOLLOW HIS PERFECT PLAN.

PLEDGE...

I WILL PUT GOD FIRST
AND HE WILL CROWN MY EFFORTS WITH SUCCESS.
I WILL SQUASH VAIN PRIDE AND HAUGHTINESS
AND GIVE GOD ONLY MY BEST.
I WILL NOT BE CONCEITED, TRAPPED IN MY OWN WISDOM
WITHOUT REVERENCE FOR OUR LORD.
I ACKNOWLEDGE THAT TITHING OF INCOME,
TIME AND TALENTS
WILL GAIN HEAVENLY REWARD.
AS A BLESSED AND HIGHLY FAVORED WOMEN OF GOD...

WHEN I LACK WISDOM...I WILL JUST ASK.

FOR THIS KNOWLEDGE WITH UNDERSTANDING
WILL AID IN COMPLETION OF ANY TASK.
I WILL STRIVE TO REPAY MY DEBTS
AND NOT SAY "SOME OTHER TIME.
I WILL NOT ENGAGE IN FIGHTING ABOUT
ISSUES THAT HAVE NO REASON OR RHYME.
AS A BLESSED AND HIGHLY FAVORED WOMEN OF GOD.
I WILL NOT BE VIOLENT OR ENVY OTHERS.
I WILL SHARE LOVE TO ALL...
NOT ONLY TO MY "SISTERS AND BROTHERS."
I WILL STUDY GOD'S WORD, BE LED BY HIS SPIRIT,
IN RENDERING SPIRITUAL ADVISEMENT...
FOR NO FAVOR WILL BE GIVEN BY GOD
IF I "SHARE" IN ADVERTISEMENT.
I AM BLESSED AND HIGHLY FAVORED
BECAUSE OF GOD'S FORGIVENESS...AND HIS GRACE...
SO, I RISE...IN HUMBLE ACCEPTANCE
TO RECEIVE "GOD'S SPECIAL PLACE."
BLESSED AND HIGHLY FAVORED!
HALLELUJAH....AMEN

BECOMING
A PROVERBS 31 WOMAN
IS NOT
ABOUT BEING "PERFECT."
IT'S ABOUT
LIVING LIFE
WITH PURPOSE,
DILIGENCE,
FORGIVENESS,
AND REPENTANCE.

SUNSET VIEW

IS THERE A "SUNSET" VIEW IN YOUR SIGHT?
THE SETTING DOWN OF HEALTH STATUS,
RELATIONSHIPS, MANIFESTATION OF DREAMS
VEERING TO THE LEFT INSTEAD OF TO THE RIGHT?
THE SONG SAYS ABOUT SUNSET...
"DAY IS DYING IN THE WEST."
BUT WAIT...STAND STILL,
THEN TURN SLOWLY,
EXPECTANTLY,
GOD STILL KNOWS FOR US, WHAT IS BEST.

AFTER SUNSET COMES THE MORNING.
TURN TO THE EAST...LOOK TO THE SUNRISE.
YES, TURN FROM THE WEST TO THE EAST.
VIEW NOW...NEW HOPE...RISING IN THE SKIES.
HOPE FOR BETTER HEALTH...
HEALING, EITHER HERE OR IN GLORY.

SOME RELATIONSHIPS ARE PUTRID AND SHOULD
BE SET DOWN. THAT IS THE REALITY OF THE STORY.
THERE ARE THINGS WE HAVE ENVISIONED
WITHOUT A PROCESS OF HOW TO ATTAIN.
THESE VISIONS MAY ACTUALLY ONLY BE DREAMS,
LIKE SKIPPING HAPHAZARDLY THROUGH THE RAIN.

THERE IS BEAUTY IN THE EVENING SUNSET.
THERE IS BEAUTY IN THE EARLY MORNING SUN RISE.
SUNSET SYMBOLIZES AN ENDING,
OR RESOLUTION OF THINGS...

WHILE SUNRISE, A NEW BEGINNING,
WITHOUT THE ATTACHMENT OF OLD STRINGS.
SO, VALUE ... REMEMBER... THE SUNSET.
ENJOY ... EMBRACE... THE SUNRISE.
FOR IT'S A SUNSET VIEW
FOR IT'S A GAME OF FAITH
WITH AN ETERNAL PRIZE.

Call to Discipleship

TO MY LOVED ONES....AND OTHERS...

AS WINTER APPROACHES I JUST STILL FEEL COMPELLED TO PLEAD AND PRAY THAT THESE WORDS WILL MEAN SOMETHING TO EACH OF MY LOVED ONES BEFORE IT'S TOO LATE. MORE AND MORE I REALIZE HOW SHORT OUR TIME IS HERE WITH OUR LOVED ONES AND IT JUST DOESN'T SEEM FAIR IF WE CAN'T BE SURE THAT WE'LL ALL MEET AGAIN IN ETERNITY. DON'T GET FED UP WITH ME... JUST ASK GOD IN PRAYER IF YOUR TIME IS NOW TO GO ALL THE WAY WITH HIM.

I LOVE YOU AND AM SO CONCERNED AS EACH DAY PASSES. ANY CHURCH THAT TEACHES THE BIBLE WILL DO AND WE ARE SURROUNDED BY THEM EVERYWHERE. JUST CHOOSE ONE TO LEARN MORE ABOUT GOD...THEN YOU'LL WANT TO GO ALL THE WAY WITH HIM. WE'RE ALL STILL LEARNING EVERY DAY OF OUR LIVES. WE'RE ALL SINNERS SAVED BY THE GRACE OF GOD. WE ALL HAVE HABITS THAT DON'T ALWAYS PLEASE HIM. BUT ONCE WE ACCEPT HIM AND LEARN MORE OF HIS WORD IT'S JUST NORMAL TO WANT TO BE BAPTIZED JUST BECAUSE HE SAID IT IN HIS WORD. HE HAS PROMISED TO FORGIVE US EVERY TIME WE ASK HIM AND THAT'S WHY I LOVE HIM SO MUCH AND WANT ALL OF MY FAMILY AND OTHERS TO BE "IN THE ARK OF SAFETY" WHILE WE HAVE A CHANCE.

I REALIZE THAT YOU'RE A "GOOD PERSON" BUT GOOD IS NOT ENOUGH WHEN GOD CALLS HIS ROLL...LOOK AROUND...GOD IS CALLING HIS ROLL. DON'T JUST TAKE CARE OF YOUR FAMILY AND THINGS, IT'S TIME TO TAKE CARE OF YOUR SOUL. ONLY BECAUSE I LOVE YOU AND AM CONCERNED ABOUT YOUR FUTURE

JOHN 14:6 NEW KING JAMES VERSION

JESUS SAID TO HIM, "I AM THE WAY, THE TRUTH, AND THE LIFE. NO ONE COMES TO THE FATHER EXCEPT THROUGH ME.

GOD IS CALLING YOU!

IN THE NIGHT SEASONS, GOD IS CALLING YOU!
IN THE QUIET CALM OF EVENING.
IN THE SNOWSTORMS THAT ARE FRIGHTENING
IN THE THUNDER AND THE LIGHTENING...
IN THE SONGS OF THE BIRDS
IN MUSICAL NOTES AND WORDS. GOD IS CALLING YOU!
WHY, BECAUSE JESUS IS COMING BACK AGAIN BY WAY OF
THE CLOUDS...THE TRUMP WILL SOUND AND THE DEAD
IN CHRIST WILL RISE FIRST...
THEN THOSE WHO REMAIN WILL BE CAUGHT UP TOGETHER
WITH HIM IN THE AIR...GET READY, JESUS IS COMING AGAIN.
THROUGH SPORTS AND PROGRAMS ON T.V.
THROUGH THE LIVES AND DEATHS OF OTHERS
HE WANTS YOU NOW...HIS GRACE TO SEE...
GOD IS CALLING YOU!
LOOK UP IN PRAISE AND GIVE THANKS.
LOOK UP, LOOK UP TOWARDS THE STARS.
HE WANTS YOU TO COME JUST AS YOU ARE!
GOD IS CALLING YOU.!.
THERE ARE NO PREPARATIONS YOU CAN MAKE...
ONLY ONE STEP YOU MUST TAKE
BE HONESTLY SORRY FOR YOUR SIN
BELIEVE IN HIS BIRTH, DEATH, RESURRECTION
THEN JUST INVITE JESUS IN.
DON'T WAIT TO BREAK BAD HABITS.
HE WILL HELP YOU TO GET RE ESTABLISHED.
DON'T WAIT TO BE PERFECT.
HIS SPIRIT WILL LEAD AND GUIDE.
HIS PROMISE IS TO BE FOREVER BY YOUR SIDE.
HE WILL GIVE YOU INNER PEACE
ALTHOUGH ALL TRIALS WILL NOT CEASE.
JESUS IS COMING...GOD IS CALLING YOU.
THROUGH HIS WORD HE SPEAKS TO YOU.
YIELD TO HIS CALL. HIS PROMISE IS TO SEE YOU THROUGH.
THROUGH ALL OF YOUR LIFE'S EXPERIENCES.
GOD IS STILL CALLING YOU.
LISTEN MY FRIEND, LISTEN....JESUS IS COMING BACK AGAIN.
GOD IS CALLING YOU!

PHILLIPIANS 2:13

"FOR IT IS GOD WHO WORKS IN YOU TO WILL AND TO ACT ACCORDING TO HIS GOOD PURPOSE."

WHAT DO WE DO WHEN WE DON'T FEEL LIKE OBEYING? GOD HAS NOT LEFT US ALONE IN OUR STRUGGLES TO DO HIS WILL. HE WANTS TO COME ALONGSIDE US AND BE WITHIN US TO HELP. GOD HELPS US WANT TO OBEY HIM AND THEN GIVES US THE POWER TO DO WHAT HE WANTS. THE SECRET TO A CHANGED LIFE IS TO SUBMIT TO GOD'S CONTROL AND LET HIM WORK. NEXT TIME, ASK GOD TO HELP YOU TO DO HIS WILL. TO BE LIKE CHRIST, WE MUST TRAIN OURSELVES TO THINK LIKE CHRIST. TO CHANGE OUR DESIRES TO BE MORE LIKE CHRIST'S, WE NEED THE POWER OF THE INDWELLING HOLY SPIRIT, THE INFLUENCE OF FAITHFUL CHRISTIANS, OBEDIENCE TO GOD'S WORD (NOT JUST EXPOSURE TO IT), AND SACRIFICIAL SERVICE. OFTEN IT IS IN DOING GOD'S WILL THAT WE GAIN THE DESIRE TO DO IT. DO WHAT GOD WANTS...TRUST HIM TO CHANGE YOUR DESIRES.
                    (LIFE APPLICATION BIBLE)

TAKE ONE MORE STEP

IF YOU'VE REPENTED OF YOUR SINS AND
ACCEPTED JESUS AS YOUR LORD
WHY NOT TAKE ONE MORE STEP
ACCORDING TO GOD'S WORD.
WHEN WE ACCEPT HIM
AS OUR SAVIOR AND OUR FRIEND
HIS WORD SAYS WE SHOULD TRUST AND OBEY
UNTIL THE VERY END.
THE WORD SAYS "REPENT AND BE BAPTIZED
EVERYONE OF YOU" GOD'S PROMISES ARE
"UNTO YOU" AND "UNTO YOUR CHILDREN TOO"
STOP AND THINK ABOUT IT…
OUR TIME ON EARTH MIGHT NOT BE LONG.
WHY NOT TAKE ONE MORE STEP…
WHILE YOU'RE STILL HEALTHY AND STRONG.
WHAT AN AWFUL THOUGHT
WHAT TERRIBLE…HORRIBLE PAIN…
WOULD BE INFLICTED ON YOUR LOVED ONES
IF GOD'S PARDON… YOU REFUSE TO GAIN.
SO… PLEASE…MY FRIEND … IF YOU HAVE REPENTED
AND ACCEPTED CHRIST AS YOUR LORD.
WHY NOT BE BAPTIZED…
TAKE ONE MORE STEP
IN OBEDIENCE TO GOD'S WORD.
ACTS 2:38,39, & 41a
"THEN PETER SAID UNTO THEM,
REPENT AND BE BAPTIZED
EVERY ONE OF YOU
IN THE NAME OF JESUS CHRIST FOR
THE REMISSION OF SINS,
AND YE SHALL RECEIVE THE GIFT
OF THE HOLY GHOST.FOR THE PROMISE IS UNTO YOU AND TO
YOUR CHILDREN, AND TO ALL THAT ARE AFAR OFF. EVEN AS
MANY AS THE LORD OUR GOD SHALL CALL
THEN THEY THAT
GLADLY RECIEVED HIS WORD.WERE BAPTIZED.

MAN BORN OF A WOMAN

HEAVENLY FATHER,
MAN WAS BORN OF A WOMAN
TO BE ON EARTH FOR ONLY A FEW DAYS.
DURING THAT TIME
YOU HAVE ADMONISHED
THAT WE CHOOSE TO WALK IN YOUR WAY.
LET US NOT TAKE LIGHTLY
THE CHOICE YOU HAVE GIVEN US
TO ACCEPT YOU AS OUR SAVIOR,
TO BE BAPTIZED,
TO OBEY
AND TO TRUST.
THERE'S NO DOUBT LORD,
THAT YOU SAID IN YOUR HOLY WORD
THERE ARE CONSEQUENCES TO BE PAID
FOR NOT
ACKNOWLEDGING YOU AS OUR LORD.
IN PHAROH'S DAY, YOU
TURNED HIM OVER TO A REPROBATE MIND
HARDENING HIS HEART SO, NO PEACE COULD HE FIND.
PEACE THAT PASSETH UNDERSTANDING
IS AN AWESOME GIFT FROM YOU.
WITHOUT PEACE OUR NUMBERED DAYS
CAN BE MOST MISERABLE...IT IS TRUE.
INNER MISERY
IS NOT
ALWAYS VISIBLE TO OTHERS
WE HAVE FOUND.
BUT INNER PEACE IS OBVIOUS
WHERE TRUE LOVE OF YOU ABOUNDS.
INNER PEACE CANNOT BE MEASURED
BY OBVIOUS CIRCUMSTANCES OF LIFE.
THE DEMON OF DARKNESS
IS ALWAYS WORKING TO STIR UP WRATH
AND EMOTIONAL STRIFE. BUT THROUGH IT ALL GOD'S PLAN
PROVIDES
PERFECT INNER PEACE AS WE CLIMB...
MOUNTAINS OF DISTRESS, JOY, SORROWS
OR MULTITUDES OF BLESSINGS.

HE GIVES PERSEVERANCE, ENDURANCE,
EMOTIONAL BALANCE
TO UPHOLD US DURING LIFE'S TESTINGS.
HIS WORD PROVIDES TO US AN AVENUE OF PRAISE.
OUR FATHER INHABITS THE PRAISE OF HIS PEOPLE
AS BLOOD CLEANSED HOLY HANDS, WE RAISE.

WE NEED NOT BE PERFECT
TO RAISE HOLY HANDS TO HIM.
PERFECTION IS NOT IN US.
WE'RE JUST SEPARATE,
FORGIVEN FROM OUR SIN.
ONLY THROUGH GOD'S FORGIVENESS
PURCHASED ON THAT OLD RUGGED CROSS
DO WE HAVE A RIGHT TO PRAISE
IN CONFIRMATION OF THE SIN THAT HE TOSSED...
AS FAR AS THE EAST IS FROM THE WEST?
THE PSALMIST DAVID SAYS...
NOT REMEMBERED, NOT RETRIEVABLE.
IT'S TIME OUR HOLY HANDS TO RAISE.

MAN BORN OF A WOMAN
HAS ONLY A FEW DAYS...
LET US WORSHIP
AND SERVE OUR CREATOR
AS WE OFFER GRATITUDE AND PRAISE

THE TIME IS NOW

THANK YOU, FATHER,
THAT INNER PEACE
AND SALVATION IS IN YOUR POWER.
THAT REPROBATE MINDS CAN BE PREVENTED BY
ACCEPTANCE OF YOU,
THIS VERY HOUR.
SATAN WANTS US TO BELIEVE
THAT THERE WILL ALWAYS BE TIME.
AND THAT ACCEPTING YOU NOW
IS NOT NECESSARY
ESPECIALLY IN YOUR PRIME.
BUT "SATAN IS A LIAR"
IT IS STATED IN GOD'S BOOK.
PROCRASTINATION
IS HIS WEAPON TO
PREVENT OUR TAKING
THAT SECOND LOOK...
INTO A LIFE THAT'S PLANNED AND DIRECTED
BECAUSE OF OUR CHOICE.
WE CAN BE COVERED BY HIS CLEANSING BLOOD
ONLY IF WE OBEY OUR SAVIOR'S VOICE.
GOD SPEAKS TO US CLEARLY
THROUGH THE PAGES OF HIS HOLY WORD.
THERE'S AN ANSWER
TO ALL OF LIFE'S QUESTIONS
REVEALED TO US...
AFTER
WE ACCEPT HIM AS LORD.
SO, WE CAN PRAISE GOD TODAY
AS WE WITNESS MANIFESTATION
OF THE PROMISES IN HIS WORD.
REMEMBER, LOVE IS ETERNAL
ONLY APPLIES
TO THOSE WHO HAVE
ACCEPTED JESUS AS LORD
LOVE THEN TRANSCENDS
TIME AND SPACE

AS WE'RE GIVEN OUR HEAVENLY REWARD.
THE TIME IS NOW, PLEASE,
NO LONGER DELAY.
COME TO HIM
WITH FAULTS AND FAILURES.
LET GOD STRAIGHTEN YOUR WAY.
WE ARE NOT PHYSICALLY OR
EMOTIONALLY ABLE
TO LIVE HOLY IN THIS LAND
PRIOR TO ACCEPTING THE SAVIOR
SO THAT ON HIS RIGHTEOUSNESS
WE CAN STAND.
EVEN THEN THERE'S NO PROMISE THAT LIFE WILL BE
PERFECT FOR YOU.
ONLY THAT IN HIM WE HAVE THE ABILITY TO GO THROUGH...
ALL THAT LIFE DEMANDS INCLUDING THE FICKLENESS OF
MAN'S HEART.
GOD DIRECTS UNMERITED GRACE
AS A BRAND NEW LIFE, WE START.
OH...COME TO THE SAVIOR.
PLEASE DELAY NO MORE.
THERE IS MERCY,
GRACE
AND PARDON
IF YOU'LL JUST OPEN YOUR HEART'S DOOR.
COME NOW...COME NOW.
MAN BORN OF A WOMAN
HAS ONLY A FEW DAYS.
SO, INVITE HIM IN NOW.
PLEASE, THERE'S NO TIME
FOR FURTHER DELAY.
THE TIME IS NOW!

TELL THEM

SOMETIMES WE'RE TOO BUSY "LIVING"
TO OFFER TO OTHERS THE "GIFT OF LIFE."
TO WARN THEM THAT TIME PASSES SWIFTLY.
OFTEN THE DOOR OF OPPORTUNITY
DOES NOT KNOCK TWICE!
WE'RE BUSY WITH FAMILY, WITH JOBS,
WITH "CHURCH WORK," WITH FRIENDS…
NEVER STOPPING TO REMIND OTHERS
THAT LIFE HERE WILL SURELY END.
TOO BUSY TO **TELL THEM** OF THE BIRTH,
LIFE, DEATH, RESURRECTION,
ASCENSION OF JESUS CHRIST.
WE THINK
JUST LIVING "A GOOD LIFE" IN THEIR PRESENCE
WILL SOMEHOW SUFFICE.
OH, MY FRIENDS,
MY FAMILY,
MY ACQUAINTANCES…
THAT IS JUST NOT ENOUGH!
LIFE'S CIRCUMSTANCES MIGHT BE EASY NOW
BUT THEY WILL AT TIMES GET PRETTY ROUGH.
TELL THEM…
THAT LIFE DOES NOT
END AT THE GRAVE.
WHERE WE SPEND ETERNITY
IS DETERMINED BY HOW WE BEHAVE….
IF OUR BEHAVIOR DOES NOT INCLUDE
ACCEPTANCE OF JESUS AS PERSONAL SAVIOR,
ETERNAL LIFE WILL NOT BE OURS…
WE WILL NOT RECEIVE GOD'S FAVOR.
THE CLOCK IS TICKING!
WE WHO KNOW THE LORD
ARE RESPONSIBLE TO TELL OTHERS.
TELL THEM…
SALVATION IS A GIFT OF LIFE…NOT EARNED!
PAID "ONCE FOR ALL" …
FOR ALL SISTERS AND BROTHERS.

GOD'S SALVATION
IS RIGHT IN FRONT OF YOU.
HE WILL COME WHEREVER YOU ARE.
TELL THEM…
SALVATION IS AS CLOSE AS
YOUR OWN MOUTH AND YOUR OWN HEART.
TELL THEM…
IT'S NOT A COMPLICATED PROCESS.
IF YOU BELIEVE IN YOUR HEART AND SAY
WITH YOUR MOUTH THAT
CHRIST IS THE RISEN LORD,
YOU WILL BE SAVED…
READ YOUR BIBLE AND PRAY.
TELL THEM…
THEY CAN THEN TALK TO GOD AS "FATHER"
RATHER THAN JUST CREATOR.
THEY CAN TRUST HIS HOLY WORD.
FOR NOW …HE IS THEIR LORD AND SAVIOR.
THEN REJOICE WITH THEM
AS YOU LET THEM KNOW
THAT EVEN THE ANGELS
REJOICE IN THE SALVATION OF THEIR SOUL
TELL THEM…
TO READ THE BIBLE.
THE BOOK OF JOHN IS A GOOD START.
ALSO, TO FIND A BIBLE BELIEVING CHURCH WHERE THEY CAN
GROW AND TAKE PART
IN PRAISE AND WORSHIP
FOR THE BEGINNING OF LIFE ANEW…
A LIFE WITH DIVINE PURPOSE.
GOD WILL NEVER LEAVE YOU.
THEN **TELL THEM**…
NOT TO BE TOO BUSY "LIVING"
TO OFFER TO OTHERS
"THE GIFT OF LIFE"
AS TIME PASSES SWIFTLY.
OPPORTUNITY
MIGHT
NOT
KNOCK TWICE!

TIME DOES NOT
BELONG
TO US
BUT MEMORIES DO
IF IN GOD WE TRUST.
HE'LL ALLOW THEM TO GENTLY
FLOW
THROUGH YOUR MIND
TO ENHANCE YOUR
HEALING PROCESS
WHICH HE COMPLETES
IN HIS TIME.